Lighting the Path to God's Presence in You

Bill Jernigan

Copyright 2018 Bill Jernigan

All rights reserved.

ISBN: 13: 978-0-9997731-1-6

ISBN 10: 0-9997731-1-9

DEDICATION

This book is dedicated to my friends and family for helping me to see the Light of Christ throughout the years that has been responsible for my own spiritual growth and maturing process.

Without the Light of Jesus, the path for my life would have had more bumps, turns and possibly dead ends. But, thanks to the Lord He has guided my life in the Light of His truth.

I am eternally indebted to my Lord Jesus Christ for giving me the opportunities and Christ-centered men that have taught me, been a Christ-like example and been a positive influence

CONTENTS

	Acknowledgments	i
	Introduction	1
1	Time Before Light	3
2	God's Light Illuminates the Way	14
3	Darkness Prevents Us From Seeing the Way	32
4	Walking in the Shadows is Costly	53
5	The Light Comes to Us	68
6	Walk in the Light of God	80
7	How Can I Walk in the Light of God?	87
8	Understanding God's Love For Us	107
9	God Comes to Live in Us	145
10	How to Light the Path of God's Presence in You	155
11	Taking God's Light into Your Community	164
12	Our Oneness in the Light	190
	Afterword	195
	About the Author	199
	From the Author's Heart	200
	Notes	201
	Appendix I (Taking the Light into the Community)	202
	Appendix II (Ministry Action Plan)	210
	Helpful Resources	211

ACKNOWLEDGMENTS

I wish to thank a dear friend, a loving brother and one who has sat under my teachings for nearly twenty years, Mark Page, who also served as editor for this work. His tireless time and efforts have helped bring this work to completion.

There is, for me, a biblical example of true brotherly friendship in the Old Testament. It was the connection God made between Jonathan, King Saul's son and David, the next King of Israel. Jonathan was willing to give his friend, David, his all. Mark has been such a friend.

INTRODUCTION

Light has historically been one of the most important human creature comforts throughout time. Without light our day ends in darkness and we grope through the night.

Have you ever awakened in the middle of the night either because the electricity has gone out or a bulb has gone out? I cannot tell you how many times that has happened to us. Our home's electric lines are owned and operated by a company whose equipment must be aged because it is not completely reliable. We can come home anytime of the day or night and find our clocks blinking. The first question we ask is, "How long was the juice out this time?"

Walking anywhere in total and absolute darkness is at the least inconvenient and at the most dangerous. Have you walked through your house when the electricity is out, and the neighborhood is as dark as a cavern? One might step on the cat's tail or worse have a surprise meeting with a piece of furniture with one's toe.

Walking through life without the Light of God is more dangerous than any inconvenient outage of electricity. Walking in the darkness of life can be down-right costly to one's life and aimless.

The Light of God represents His presence and His hope. Darkness represents the opposite, the absence of God and the lack of hope.

I will attempt to walk you through the theological idea of walking in the Light of God, not from a highly technical standpoint but lighter to make it easy to understand.

So many people walk in the darkness. There are a great number of people walking in the shadows of God's light. They are not walking in total darkness, but neither are they walking in the brilliance of God's light. They are somewhere in-between.

My prayer for you is that you will discover the Light that gives your life victory, power, direction and will give you the hope for tomorrow.

All Scriptures is from the New American Standard Version unless otherwise stated.

1 TIME BEFORE LIGHT

"The earth was formless and void, and darkness was over the surface of the deep, and the Spirit of God was moving over the surface of the waters. (Genesis 1:2)

You might want to read this statement, close your eyes and use your imagination. Imagine for a moment that there is absolutely no light – at all! What do you see? Without the light one can see nothing. Now turn on light and what do you see? You will see beautiful colors, shapes, and objects.

Darkness is the absence of light. Light cancels darkness.

Now there are those who will have difficulty with this entire idea because our modern, enlightened and technologically advanced society has a problem with a five-letter word: F.A.I.T.H. This type of person operates in an almost scientific realm where something must be able to be observed, measured, quantified and proven.

> ***Faith requires no proof***

FAITH requires no proof. The writer of the New Testament book of Hebrews more than adequately defines faith in Hebrews 11:1, "Now faith is being sure of what we hope for and certain of what we do not see. (NIV) The New Century Version states this verse this way, "Faith means being sure of the things we hope for and knowing that something is real even if we do not see it."

Faith is like knowing something without any proof what–so–ever. Let me use a few examples.

A couple marries because of love, not because of proof they will spend a lifetime of bliss in each other's arms. No matter what, they both believe their marriage will work. Ask the couple to prove their love and you will get a surprised look.

If you get into your car, aboard a ship or plane to take a journey, you do so by faith. Oh, you may not realize faith is at work, but how do you know you will safely arrive at your destination? In any of these modes of transportation there could be mechanical breakdown or an accident. What thought do you give to the physical condition of the pilot flying the aircraft? In all of these situations, you do so being "sure of what you hope for."

Now look back at the biblical definition of faith in Hebrews 11:1. "Now faith is being sure of what we hope for and certain of what we do not see." Human beings operate many times throughout each day in a hope that something will happen according to what we need or want.

Faith operates in the space of trust. We enter marriage trusting our perspective spouse. We trust the aircraft will deliver us safely to our destination. We trust our automobile will crank and stop on our trip. And somehow, we trust the driver in the other car racing towards us at 70 miles per hour, that the small yellow (white) line between us will keep us safe.

This explanation is a building block to the entire book. Without faith in the Scriptures and God who breathed life into them, you will not comprehend anything between the covers.

My prayer for you is, "Dear Heavenly Father, Your Word teaches us, 'without faith it is impossible to please Him (You), for he who comes to God must believe that He is and that He is a rewarder of those who seek Him' (You). (Hebrews 11:6) We are each in a great need to trust you more today than we did yesterday. I earnestly ask that You, Lord to reveal Yourself in a way that we will trust You more and our faith in You may be deepened. May we read this work with an open mind and a tender heart for Your Truth." Amen.

Again, it is the time to use your imagination. We must begin before the beginning of anything. We must go to a time before creation. This takes faith. Even scientist cannot find an explanation or agree on our beginnings. You might be amazed to hear me say, "I don't know the "how", but I know the "Who."

We know that God, the Creator, gave Moses the books of Genesis, Exodus, Leviticus, Numbers and Deuteronomy. These five books of the Old Testament are collectively called, "The Torah". In the book of Genesis, chapter 1, verse 1 we see, *In the beginning God created the heavens and the earth.* This verse answers the "Who"- God (Yahweh or Jehovah). Christians should not be overwhelmed by attempting to explain the "how" creation was achieved, only the "Who". This takes blind faith but there are more important issues to deal with rather than struggling over how creation occurred. Here is a point that helped me, personally, no matter how God accomplished creation is the fact that He wanted to create you and I to have a close, loving relationship with Him and depend upon Him with all of our hearts.

God told Moses in verse two, *"The earth was formless and void, and darkness was over the surface of the deep, and the Spirit of God was moving over the surface of the waters."* Important words to focus upon in this verse are "formless", "void", and "dark". The idea is there was absolutely nothing. The whole universe was a blank.

This truth is difficult for the modern world to comprehend. It is difficult to imagine nothing, isn't it? If you were to travel to a deep dark cavern, wore blinders to cancel all light, you would still have sound, smell, taste and touch. Let's say you could cancel out light and sound, what about the three other senses: smell, taste and touch?

For argument's sake, let's imagine you could cancel out all of your senses. What do you think you would find? Nothing! What about the air you breathe? If you were to cancel out air you'd definitely have a short time to live. Get the point – nothing. You would be dead. There would not even be thoughts left in your body.

The Latin word for the pre-creation is "ex-hilio". God took nothing and created all there is or will ever be by speaking it into existence. From nothing God created space, all of the heavenly bodies, the law of physics (which God uses today to hold things together), our world and all that is on it including every kind of life. I would say this idea is tough to explain. Wouldn't you?

What does creation reveal about God? Creation reveals:

1. His wisdom and power (Job 28:23–27; Proverbs 3:19);

2. His glory (Psalm 19:1);

3. His power and Godhead (Romans 1:18–21);

4. His love for an insignificant man (Psalm 8:3–9);

5. His providential care (Isaiah 40:12ff). Our Lord, when on earth, saw the gracious hand of the Father even in the flowers and fowl (Matthew 6:25ff).[1]

The words "formless and void" indicates the world was in a state of confusion and empty. One from a science background one might say, "All of the molecules and atoms were there, but not yet organized into the form of anything. Yet there was "nothing". No atoms, no molecules, just God. He would work an additional five days to organize and complete His creation.

So, why attempt to explain God? If you spent every heart-beating moment of your life from birth to death trying to understand and explain God, you wouldn't be able to understand any more than a molecule of a realization who and what God is. So why attempt? Why waste your life when it is much easier to accept God at His Word?

In verses 3-5, God told Moses, Then God said, *"Let there be light"; and there was light. God saw that the light was good; and God separated the light from the darkness. God called the light day, and the darkness He called night. And there was evening and there was morning, one day.*

This is the point in which the discussion of this book begins. We must begin to understand from the beginning the idea and truth about "light".

Light and darkness are at opposite ends of the spectrum. Take two vehicles, one white and one black. What do they have in common? Nothing? Well, both are colors of the spectrum in common. The color white is actually seen by our eyes as the reflection of all of the colors of the light spectrum, while black is the absorption of all light by our eyes of the light of the spectrum. That is why a black car is much hotter in the sun than a white car.

It is strange for us to consider that God separated the light from darkness, but this is a cosmological or astronomical idea. In other words, there would be day and there would be night. In verse 5 God called the light day, a term we still use to this day and He called darkness, night. In verse 4 He pronounced the light as "good".

Now that is the foundation for our world from nothingness to the creation of light, we will need to move on about God and His light through time. There are 218 different verses in the Old and New Testament concerning light.

God's creative work with light was not over. In Genesis 1:14-15, God revealed to Moses the next step in creating light. We read, "Then God said, *'Let there be lights in the expanse of the heavens to separate the day from the night, and let them be for signs and for seasons and for days and years; and let them be for lights in the expanse of the heavens to give light on the earth'; and it was so.*"

This account of creation points toward God's creation of the lights of the stars in heaven. Isn't it interesting to consider that He created Earth first, then the rest of the universe? If you can accept this by faith, then you might understand why Christians and Jews consider our world as the center of God's creation. In addition, He created this world for the inhabitation of the crown of His creation – man.

The "lights in the expanse" gives us the fact of God's creation of the rest of the universe. In general, verses 14-15 is where we have light. The command given concerning them: Let there be lights in the firmament of heaven. God had said, Let there be light (v. 3), and there was light; but this was, as it were, a chaos of light, scattered and confused: now it was collected and modelled, and made into several luminaries, and so rendered both more glorious and more serviceable.[2]

The second reference to "light in the expanse" to separate the day from night, (verses 14-15) we see God's order beginning to come together. God is order, never chaos. "The lights were to be in the firmament of heaven, that vast expanse which encloses the earth, and is conspicuous to all".[3]

The lights of the expanse would illuminate the evening sky, but this light was inadequate to light the earth. Now, let me remind you of a historical point: these lights in the firmament are extremely important to life on earth and specifically for man's purposes. The points of light in the evening sky are fixed and always in the same relative position. I am not speaking as a scientist, but as one who is generally knowledgeable of the use of stars. All navigation on earth, either by air or sea has used the stars fixed relative position to navigate their vessels. Imagine how impossible it would be to go long distances from point A to point B without the navigation by stars. So, this light is somewhat guiding lights for a journey. Of course, now navigation is done by Global Position Satellites. But one can look to the evening sky and be able to discern compass direction.

One huge use of the light of the firmament was the birth announcement of Jesus. In the Gospel of Matthew, we read about the firmament's announcement of the birth of Jesus. *"Now after Jesus was born in Bethlehem of Judea in the days of Herod the king, magi from the east arrived in Jerusalem, saying,* **"Where is He who has been born King of the Jews? For we saw His star in the east and have come to worship Him."** (Matthew 2:1-2) This light in the heavens famously guided the magi to the birth of the King of Kings and Lord of Lords.

The lights of the firmament have been studied for thousands of years. In an article for Sciencing.com, Julie Ackendorf reported the use of the stars by ancient people by writing "Long before the ancient peoples of the Earth utilized the stars and plants to figure out when to plant and harvest their crops, they named the constellations – most of which are still in use today – and told stories about the heroes and gods, animals and mythological creatures represented in the stars. Besides the entertainment factor, these stories about the stars helped ancient storytellers teach both young and old, preserve their cultures and instill moral values into the tribe's citizens."[4]

In God's order He had to have known these tiny points of light would be highly useful to mankind. All of God's creation was spoken into existence for a reason and for man's use. They are not in the sky either by accident or without purpose.

The specs of light in the heavens also distinguish night from day. Let me give you another reason of non-spiritual application of this great gift from God. Think of all of the poetry and songs written about the inspiration of the stars not to mention how they've influenced romance. How much has been written about a starless, dark night.

One night I sat on our patio. As I looked into the heavens and noticed the great points of light I realized they each represented planets, suns and constellations. Astronomers and NASA have given us fantastic glimpses of what lies beyond our vision into outer space. Each is unique and beautiful in its own way. As I sat there, knowing Almighty God had created each and every one of these heavenly bodies all with different properties and sizes, I wept in worship of our Heavenly Father. I felt such awe at His creation's immensity and my own insignificance compared to His creation. As I sat there I prayed, "Dear God, when I see what You've created by the power of Your spoken word compared to my insignificance and yet You are so mindful of me as a person, my needs and my feelings, I am caught in complete and total thanksgiving and awe of Your great love for me and humanity."

> *On the fourth day, God created our world's sun and moon.* (Genesis 1:16-19)

"God made the two great lights, the greater light to govern the day, and the lesser light to govern the night; He made the stars also. God placed them in the expanse of the heavens to give light on the earth, and to govern the day and the night, and to separate the light from the darkness; and God saw that it was good. There was evening and there was morning, a fourth day."

Our star, the sun, is known to be 93 million miles from earth. It sits in the center of our solar system with all the eight planets revolving around its life-giving radiance. The distance of the earth from the sun is known by scientist as the "Goldilocks Zone" because if the earth were any closer, we would be incinerated and any further away it would be a frozen wasteland. God put us at the right distance from our sun for life to flourish on earth.

Presently scientists are looking for similar solar systems that might have a planet in the so-called Goldilocks Zone. They feel if this works on earth that it will work in other solar systems.

When we consider God's order in creation there are several factors to consider about His creation of the greater light, the sun. Our planet's position from the sun gives us several blessings:

- needed warmth for comfort and the necessary temperature for plant growth for food
- the chemical reaction between chlorophyll, carbon dioxide and sunlight to produce for needed plant food
- gives us a dependable time of sunrise and sunset, predictable and calculable
- gives us a dependable length of a solar year – 365.25 days
- marks the end of one day and the beginning of its night, with 24 hours in a day's time period
- the sun gives us light to illuminate our work

Should you consider the might, power, and forethought of our Mighty Creator, you will see how perfect His creation is and how thoughtful of us prior to the creation of humans. He made light for our benefit. Without the light we would not exist. The Psalmist wrote, *"The heavens are telling of the glory of God; and their expanse is declaring the work of His hands."* (Psalm 19:1)

The lesser light, the moon, God made to rule over the night. (verse 18) Our moon has no light of its own. It only reflects the light of the Great Light, the sun. The moon is approximately one-fourth the size of the Earth, but its tiny size has a great impact upon all of us. It rotates in an orbit of the earth at a distance of 238,900 miles.

Science classes in middle and high school teaches us that our moon does the following:

- Our closest neighbor has a great magnetic attraction upon the earth and pulls on our seas creating tides

- The moon has cycles (full moon, quarter moon, new moon, and first quarter moon) are regular and predictable

> *We see and know God through His creation.*

- Prior to our modern age the calendar was calculated by many cultures different methods.

- Scientists believe that the moon stabilizes the earth's rotation. They know the earth wobbles slightly as it spins and the moon minimizes this wobble,

- Many people working in the public swear that the full moon affects the behavior of people. Ask an Emergency Room doctor or nurse and your child's teacher. Scientists believe that since our bodies are 75% water, that our bodies are affected like the seas by the pull of the moon, called the Lunar Effect.

The two great lights in our sky have been used for many millennia for the seasonal measurement and for signs. Planting and harvest seasons were determined by the timing of the two great lights. We have a wooden fence on the backside of our yard. Over the years I have noticed the position of the sunrise and watched the sunrise travel from the southern part of the fence in the winter to the northern part of the fence in the summer. In Genesis 1:14-15 we see written, *"Then God said, "Let there be ^alights in the expanse of the heavens to separate the day from the night, and let them be for signs and for seasons and for days and years; and let them be for lights in the expanse of the heavens to give light on the earth"; and it was so."* The movement of the sunrise is a sign of the changing seasons.

The writer of the New Testament book of Romans penned this, *"For since the creation of the world His invisible attributes, His eternal power and divine nature, have been clearly seen, being understood through what has been made, so that they are without excuse."* (Romans 1:20) God clearly wanted mankind to know Him through His creation. Notice, I did not say know "about" Him, but to "know" Him. Scriptures are clear that God wants us to intimately know Him, not know facts about Him. I have an interest in history and many of my extended family members have interest in our genealogical heritage. Through their on-going research and the internet, we have discovered that my family are descendants of King Knut of Scandinavia and through he and his descendants the Danish people has given a great deal to our Anglo ancestry and history. While these Vikings were rugged and extremely brutal conquerors, I know about them, but I do not know them personally.

Ministers encounter many people that know about God, but from their lives we wonder if they've ever had a personal encounter with the Living God through His Son Jesus. We may work with them, perhaps related to them or even go to Bible study and worship with them, but only the Lord Himself knows their true spiritual condition. Scriptures definitely make a distinction between knowing about God and knowing Him.

I truly hope you know the difference. Once a man said, "People miss heaven by twelve inches, the distance between the brain and the heart." I have seen the Light! The Light has radically changed my life, my thoughts, my desires and my passions. What a Mighty

God I serve!

2 GOD'S LIGHT ILLUMINATES THE WAY

The LORD was going before them in a pillar of cloud by day to lead them on the way, and in a pillar of fire by night to give them light, that they might travel by day and by night. (Exodus 13:21)

Most of us have used a flashlight at one time or another to see our way in the darkness. When I was a young boy we lived many miles outside of a small rural town. My grandparents lived across a field about a hundred yards from our home. My siblings and I were in their home almost as much as we were in our own. Each week I would go down to my grandparent's home and watch the television show, "Gunsmoke" with Pappaw.

There was a vast difference between one hundred yards from daytime to dark. As a boy my wild imagination was alive and well. Since the only light was on the front of their house I had to travel in complete darkness aiming my journey to that one light. Many times, I could just imagine a wolf or some mammoth night-time beast waiting to eat me up. So, I would run as fast as my feet would function.

Sometimes life is that way, too. We are traveling through life filled with dark hours. In the Old Testament book of Genesis, chapter 37 – 50 the story of Joseph unfolds. For the purpose of this writing, I will compress the story greatly. Joseph was tricked and sold into bondage in Egypt. Through the years, Joseph's became powerful in Pharaoh's house.

In Exodus Egypt, Joseph's descendants grew so enormous that the new Pharaoh worried the Egyptians would be overcome by the Hebrews. Pharaoh gave instructions *"Come, let us deal wisely with them, or else they will multiply and in the event of war, they will also join themselves to those who hate us, and fight against us and depart from the land."* (Exodus 1:10)

So Pharaoh enslaved them and put them into harsh and unbearable conditions. In verses 11-14 we are given a description of Egypt's treatment of the Hebrews.

> *"So they appointed taskmasters over them to afflict them with hard labor. And they built for Pharaoh storage cities, Pithom and Raamses. But the more they afflicted them, the more The Hebrews multiplied and the more they spread out, so that they were in dread of the sons of Israel. The Egyptians compelled the sons of Israel to labor rigorously; and they made their lives bitter with hard labor in mortar and bricks and at all kinds of labor in the field, all their labors which they rigorously imposed on them."*

In the following verses we are told that Pharaoh feared the Hebrews so much that he instructed the Hebrew mid-wives to kill any male children born, but female children were allowed to live. Despite his instructions the mid-wives fearing God, did not kill the male babies.

Now begins the story of Moses. Moses escaped the death sentence by being put in a wicker basket by his mother and floated down the Nile, where Pharaoh's daughter had the infant removed from the water. She raised Moses as her own son and Moses grew up as an Egyptian.

One day Moses saw the mistreatment of one of the Hebrews by an Egyptian and killed him. (Exodus 2:10-11) We're told in verse 15 that Pharaoh heard of Moses' actions and tried to have him killed. So Moses escaped to Midian where He would have his first encounter with Jehovah God, YHWH or The Light.

While in Midian, Moses married and had a son. One day while tending his father-in-law's sheep on the west side of the wilderness, at Mt. Horeb, the Mountain of God. (Exodus 3:1) The Scriptures reveal that an angel of the Lord appeared to Moses in a burning bush. While the bush burned it was not consumed. (Exodus 3:2)

We are told that Moses looked upon the burning bush and heard a voice say, *""Moses, Moses!"* And he said, *"Here I am."* Then He (Lord) said, *"Do not come near here; remove your sandals from your feet, for the place on which you are standing is holy ground."* He said also, *"I am the God of your father, the God of Abraham, the God of Isaac, and the God of Jacob.""* (verses 4-6).

The first key to grasp is the fact that the Lord God revealed Himself in the fire of a burning bush. Obviously light was involved here for fire puts off light. In the revelation of God to Moses, Moses must have had an understanding of who God was from his ancestors and a sense of the presence of God. The appearance of God no doubt frightened Moses and in verse 6, *"Then Moses hid his face, for he was afraid to look at God"* for fire was a symbol of God's presence and would be seen again.

> ***God revealed Himself through the light of a burning bush***

Moses responded to God's instruction, with excuses as to why he couldn't accomplish what God wanted him to do. Moses did confront Pharaoh, and presented what many call plagues, but which I call judgments upon Pharaoh's house and nation. The Hebrews were eventually and reluctantly released and proceeded to cross the land headed for "The Promised Land". The Hebrews remained in bondage in Egypt for 430 years until God freed them from their bondage to Pharaoh. (12:41)

The Lord God illuminated the Hebrews journey. Remember the story I told of running at night to my grandparents' home because it was dark outside? The Hebrews were in the middle of the desert where the sun would scorch them during the day and they would experience pitch darkness during the night.

> *God provided a pillar of fire to light the way during the night*

Remember, the Hebrews were God's chosen people. He made a covenant many hundred years before with Abraham and again with Jacob and God's promises never go unfulfilled. He is the God of completion and order and never half-baked and chaos. God would lead the Hebrews on a long, difficult journey back to their homeland.

God provided the Hebrews with guidance and protection. In chapter 13 of Exodus God provided a shade during the hot day with a pillar of a cloud and in the evening, He provided a pillar of fire to light the way. (13:21-22) What a God! He didn't send them on their way. He went ahead of the group. God is not one to follow us, but it is us that should follow Him.

While on their journey the Hebrews complained over and over again. They constantly wanted to return to Egypt and resubmit themselves to treatment they previously groaned about and prayed for release. God supplied their very needs for food and water. The Lord provided the Hebrews in the middle of the desert where there was no food or water, (15:22-27) quail, (16:13) quail and manna (vs. 16:14).

The Lord showed Himself a second time to Moses by fire in Exodus19:18-21.

> *"Now Mount Sinai was all in smoke because the LORD descended upon it in fire; and its smoke ascended like the smoke of a furnace, and the whole mountain quaked violently. When the sound of the trumpet grew louder and louder, Moses spoke, and God answered him with thunder. The LORD came down on Mount Sinai, to the top of the mountain; and the LORD called Moses to the top of the mountain, and Moses went up. Then the LORD spoke to*

> *Moses, 'Go down, warn the people, so that they do not break through to the LORD to gaze, and many of them perish.'"*

This revelation was a demonstration of the power and might of the One who created light and the entire known universe. This was a historic sermon delivered not by man, but by God Himself. (Exodus 20) On top of the mountain God spoke to Moses and his brother Aaron. Yet the assembled people below heard the powerful voice of God Almighty.

It is important to stress that this was not words spoken by Moses or Aaron. The whole assembly of the Hebrews witnessed God descending upon the Mt. Sinai in fire. They witnessed the shechinah, or glory of the Lord. In verses 16-17 we see the description of a once-in-a-lifetime revelation of YHWH (pronounced Ya-way).

> **"So it came about on the third day, when it was morning, that there were thunder and lightning flashes and a thick cloud upon the mountain and a very loud trumpet sound, so that all the people who were in the camp trembled. And Moses brought the people out of the camp to meet God, and they stood at the foot of the mountain."**

The call to worship was a trumpet announcing the arrival of YHWH. When the sound of the trumpet grew louder and louder, Moses spoke and God answered him with thunder.

When God reveals Himself, it is never an ordinary event. A revelation by the Lord is first an encounter with Him. He shows Himself to a person to reveal His person, His mind, His heart, His will and His purpose.

Many people will commend a pastor for a wonderful message for his form or content, but the real question is, "How did the Word of God change your life?" A revelation from God is not for your information, which many today mistaken. God's revelation is for your transformation that leads to your participation (to be on mission with Him) and ultimately His glorification.

I would be willing to say God's voice got the assembly's attention. Imagine your eyes glued to the Glory of the Lord on Mt. Sinai. Do you think you'd be able to blink your eyes? Is it possible that you would catch your lower jaw dropping down? Would your heart be racing?

While God was speaking He gave the Hebrews His law. Let me ask you a question. Do you think God's laws are suggestions or does He mean what He says? I find that we're all guilty of ignoring God in our lives many times. Through the years as I have discovered my personal life is contrary to the Word of God, I feel rotten inside because I have let God down. I have learned to never dismiss what God's said to me but begin implementing it in my life.

Throughout history men and women from all walks of life, nations and tongues have made this commitment. When one gives one's life to Jesus in redemption, it is no longer their life to live but it from then on belongs to Jesus to do his will.

The chapter heading, "Light the Way" is meant to show you how God, the Creator of Light, has appeared and spoken to ordinary individuals. Light always illuminates our way. There are many examples one might use, but for instance take your automobile. When driving at night either you or the vehicle turns on the headlights, so you can see where you are going. Try living in a rural setting where there are no street lamps or lighting from signs. You will either depend upon your auto's headlights to steer safely down the road or you'll end up in a ditch or wrapped around a tree. Driving, whether in town or in the country, is dependent upon you safely navigating.

One's life is like driving an auto. The steering of one's life is very sensitive and a small swerve may cause one to veer where one doesn't want to veer. Spiritual distractions can be as deadly as a distraction while driving, such as texting and driving. I am addressing temptations. Our modern society has many more temptations to distract us than a generation or two ago. Each temptation may seem harmless, but one never knows where a temptation will lead. I know, you say, "I can handle that." But, you maybe or may not be able to withstand the temptation. There have been mature and well anchored believers that have been swayed by temptation. Temptations are sinful, it is one's response to a temptation is wrong in the eyes of the Lord or they wouldn't be a temptation.

The purpose of God's Word (Scriptures) is to guide us. The Psalmist wrote this, *"Your word is a lamp to my feet and a light to my path."* (Psalm 119:105) This passage gives us the fact that our lives can only be lived successfully and powerfully within the will of God as revealed in His Word. The Psalmist knew that God's Word shines light upon the path of life and is our only dependable source of truth.

Dr. Faucet said, "Not only does the Word of God inform us of His will, but, as a light on a path in darkness, it shows us how to follow the right and avoid the wrong way. The lamp of the Word is not the sun. He would blind our eyes in our present fallen state; but we may bless God for the light shining as in a dark place, to guide us until the Son of Righteousness shall come, and we shall be made capable of seeing Him (2 Peter 1:19; Revelation 22:4). The lamp is fed with the oil of the Spirit. The allusion is to the lamps and torches carried at night before an Eastern caravan.

> *God's light shows us the right path to follow*

There are several records in Scriptures concerning the light of God. The light that people saw was usually so brilliant it was almost blinding.

Jesus is The Light

Jesus was transfigured on a high mountain. In Matthew 17:1-2, we are told, *"Jesus took with Him Peter and James and John his brother and led them up on a high mountain by themselves. And He was transfigured before them; and His face shone like the sun, and His garments became as white as light."* (Also in Mark 9: 2-13 and Luke 9:28-36)

The Greek New Testament gives us a better understanding of what happened during Jesus' transfiguration. When we speak of transfigured, we actually mean "metemorphōthē" a change in form. Take for example the butterfly. It begins life as a particular type of caterpillar, it crawls. After entering a self-made cocoon, it begins to be changed or transformed into a butterfly. It enters the cocoon as one bug and exits as a totally different bug. This one is usually pretty and flies or rather flutters in the air.

Jesus walked upon a high mountain with three of His closest disciples: Peter, James and his brother John. The three disciples were personal witnesses of this extraordinary and divine occurrence. The custom of that day was to have two or more witnesses to validate just about any claim, including a crime. These three men were of great faith and highly trustworthy.

The substance of his body remained the same, but the accidents and appearances of it were greatly altered; he was not turned into a spirit, but his body, which had appeared in weakness and dishonor, now appeared in power and glory. Jesus' face glowed like the sun and his garments became white as light. (Verse 2) While addressing the issue of Jesus' transfiguration it is important to know that while Jesus walked the earth he did so as a normal human being. This may cause some of you a problem, but in Philippians 2:7, Paul wrote the

Philippian church and said, *"Christ Jesus, who, although He existed in the form of God, did not regard equality with God a thing to be grasped, but emptied Himself, taking the form of a bond-servant, and being made in the likeness of men. Being found in appearance as a man, He humbled Himself by becoming obedient to the point of death, even death on a cross.* (Philippians 2:5–8)

Jesus drew a veil over the glory of his godhead; but now, in his transfiguration, he removed the veil and appeared in the form of God (Philippians 2:6), and gave his disciples a glimpse of his glory, which could not but change his form. In our limited minds we consider that things and people are one way or another. We many times try to explain the existence of God within the framework of our human minds, when God operates outside our natural laws and understanding.

Jesus was both God and man. One must be careful not to separate the two for if one does; one is crossing the line into polytheism or more than one God or Gnosticism.

The truth of God's light permeates throughout the Old and New Testament, from Genesis 1 to Revelation 22. God is light! (I John 1:5) So, when Jesus appeared as God He did so as light.

Another example of Jesus' divine presence and appearance of light was in the call of Saul of Tarsus. (Acts 9) Saul was traveling through the region persecuting those who followed Jesus. *"As he was traveling, it happened that he was approaching Damascus, and suddenly a light from heaven flashed around him;"* (Verse 3) Saul saw the light and heard the voice of Jesus. In verses 4-6, we can see how the voice and light of Christ impacted Saul's life.

> *"And he fell to the ground and heard a voice saying to him, 'Saul, Saul, why are you persecuting Me?' And he said, 'Who are You, Lord?' And He said, 'I am Jesus whom you*

are persecuting, but get up and enter the city, and it will be told you what you must do.'"

Saul was called by name by a voice from Heaven. (Verse 5) and immediately the voice answered him by saying, "*I am Jesus whom you are persecuting.*" This was one of the earliest manifestations of "light" in the post-resurrection New Testament. An occurrence of this nature doesn't happen casually or daily. This was a supernatural encounter with the Living God. As in Genesis when Moses encountered Jehovah God in the light of the burning bush, Saul had seen the light of God and it was about to make a huge impact upon the life of Saul.

The voice of Jesus told Saul to "*get up and enter the city, and it will be told you what you must do.*" (Verse 6) The men accompanying Saul "were speechless" but saw "no one". (Verse 7) In verse 8-9, we are told of a result of Saul's encounter with Jesus, "*Saul got up from the ground, and though his eyes were open, he could see nothing; and leading him by the hand, they brought him into Damascus. And he was three days without sight, and neither ate nor drank.*"

When a person has an encounter with the Living God, the person's life is deeply impacted and never the same from that point on. At this point Saul was blinded, but soon the Lord would remove Saul's blindness and the direction of Saul's life took a turn that most people in churches today would not be too welcoming. Saul went as directed to a man named Ananias, who in a separate encounter with Jesus was told to him, "*Go, for he is a chosen instrument of Mine, to bear My name before the Gentiles and kings and the sons of Israel; for I will show him how much he must suffer for My name's sake.*" (9:15-16)

There are many other encounters with the Light in the New Testament:

In Acts Chapter 12 we see another encounter with the Light. The Apostle Peter was arrested and thrown in jail for his solid faith in Christ and willingness to remain firm in his preaching and life as he followed Christ. Incarceration isn't too uncommon for a person proclaiming the One True Living God in a pagan society. There are missionaries and relief workers today jailed, persecuted and killed on a regular basis for sharing their faith and standing firm in their beliefs.

> *an angel of the Lord suddenly appeared and a bright light shone in the prison cell*

In this chapter we see in verse one where King Herod Agrippa I, had James, the brother of John put to death with a sword and how it pleased the Jews. Herod had to be listening, like many politicians today, to opinion polls. When he heard how this pleased the Jews he decided to have Peter arrested and jailed.

The church had quickly become under persecution. Anyone identified as a "follower of Jesus" was in danger of losing their life and suffering indescribable hardships.

Now Peter wasn't simply thrown into a cell and left, but Herod had sixteen (4 squads) of Roman soldiers to guard him. These soldiers weren't a Barney Fife of Mayberry, they were crack fighting soldiers. How would you like to be a pagan and chained to Peter for an entire shift of duty?

Herod's intent was to bring Peter out before the people for a public trial as soon as Passover was over. If you will remember during Jesus' trial there was a sticky point about Jesus' crucifixion occurring during Passover. Herod could have feared this custom would arise if he tried Peter during the Passover Festival, but waiting until it was over would secure that he could proceed with Peter in any way he saw fit.

While Peter was entertaining the troops with their need for salvation, unrelentingly, the church was busy praying. There is one truth I hope to impart to you today – when stuff happens, and trials and tribulations occur, God's people discover they can kneel and pray. It has been often said of American Christians by believers in other nations, that we are not serious about our faith or prayer life because we have grown too accustomed to the "good life", without a sword or prison sentence hanging over our heads like in Africa or the old Eastern Bloc countries during the U.S.S.R. era.

Luke, the writer of Acts tells us, *"So Peter was kept in the prison, but prayer for him was being made fervently by the church to God."* (Acts 12:5) The word "fervently" is a Greek word meaning "continuously, without ceasing". Peter's church family, where ever they met, whether in homes, gardens or at the local IHOP, they prayed without ceasing.

Fervent pray is rare today. Many, many churches no longer even have a regular prayer service. They seemingly are going down a river without a divine connection, relying upon their own wisdom and desires. After the death, burial and resurrection, we see this type of prayer emphasis when the Christians were told to stay in Jerusalem. (Acts 1:4)

In James 5:16, we read,

> "The effectual fervent prayer of a righteous man availeth much.

Prayer should not be a last resort, but a first connection

> "The prayer of a righteous man is powerful and effective. (New International Version)

> "The effective prayer of a righteous man can accomplish much. (NASB)

Prayer should not be a last resort, but our first connection. Question: do you start on a journey relying upon your sense of direction and the specific roads you will take? My wife and I took out on a journey from Southeast Texas to Northwest Montana and several points before and after. I did the driving and Karen did the sightseeing. I knew the general direction of northwest, but the specific highways to get there was unknown. I had to rely upon Google Maps on my phone to give me step-by-step directions, turns and highways numbers. Without this GPS device we might have ended up in Bolivia.

The same principle applies to our daily lives. Too often we don't take the time and effort to pray, so we simply begin and ask God to bless it. Warning - God is not under any obligation, whether you are His child or not, to bless your efforts if you haven't consulted Him in "fervent prayer".

I believe there might be two or more reasons why our churches aren't spending more time in prayer. The first reason is they are not connected to the Heavenly Father by redemption through His Son, Jesus. In other words, they are lost. No matter if they've been walked the aisle, spoken to the pastor, prayed and been baptized – if you are not walking in the light of God you are not a child of God – He's not going to hear you.

The second reason is reasonably understood that people do not have a prayer life is they've not been taught. People can find it enlightening to study the prayers of God's people in the Old and New Testaments for a pattern. Jesus even taught a basic outline of prayer.

One might say what you might, but here's how I was taught to pray: A.C.T.S.

Adoration　　Jesus started out, "Our Father which are in Heaven, hallow is thy name.

There are so many ways to adore our Heavenly Father – pick one. Think about what God has done in history and what He has previously done in your life. Remember what He has given you, (family, home, job, people to love you) and don't forget redemption.

Consider His great love for you. Ponder His provisions in your life and the wonders of His creation, such as: colors, variety the sun, moon and stars. The list is endless, but I would suggest not using the same list over and over. Otherwise it become an empty liturgy rather than from your heart.

Confession　　What does one confess? It is easy and difficult. We should confess our sins, our short-falls, our weaknesses, our actions, our thoughts and every aspect of the day from awakening until going to sleep at night. An important truth to confess is what He (God) means to you and what your life would be like without Him. Confess what the Holy Spirit speaks to you about.

Confession means, "agreeing with God". The Lord reveals His character, His will, His purposes and His plans in His Word. Confession is much more than saying, "I'm sorry! For without actions, words are simply words.

Thanksgiving This should be self-explanatory. However, too many times I hear people publicly praying and they go down a list of thank-you like reading a list of cards. One should put in adoration and confession, don't you think?

Supplication We got this one down pat! Huh? This is our list of wants and desires. Give Me this, give me that, bless Aunt Sophie, and be with so and so. I personally call this "rubbing the genies lamp" instead of talking to our Heavenly Father.

Supplication could and should be a whole lot more. Shouldn't we pray for the spiritual welfare of our families, friends, relatives, co-workers and church family?

What about praying for our spiritual leaders? You know, your pastor, his staff and those who represent us across the world proclaiming Jesus.

I try to make "me" the last item. Rarely is the "me" list – "give me". I think of Solomon's prayer for wisdom and for God's truth to become real to me.

I can only imagine what was going through the minds of the followers of Jesus. They probably said something like this: "Well our Master has been crucified on the cross and buried. God raised Him from the dead and He ascended into the heavens. Now what do we do?" Luke tells us in verses 13-14, *"When they had entered the city, they went up to the upper room where they were staying; that is, Peter and John and James and Andrew, Philip and Thomas,*

Bartholomew and Matthew, James the son of Alphaeus, and Simon the Zealot, and Judas the son of James. These all with <u>one mind</u> were <u>continually devoting themselves to prayer</u>, along with the women, and Mary the mother of Jesus, and with His brothers."

Supposition aside, we're told in verse 14 what the followers of Jesus did after His ascension. They were all with one mind and continually devoting themselves to prayer. The word "continually" carries with it the same idea as "fervent". This group felt prayer was imperative. They had prayer modeled by Jesus Himself. The disciples learned from Jesus and the people probably learned from hearing Jesus pray as well as the disciples.

In Acts 12:7–18 you can read the result of the fervently praying church:

> *"And behold, an angel of the Lord suddenly appeared and a light shone in the cell; and he struck Peter's side and woke him up, saying, 'Get up quickly.' And his chains fell off his hands. And the angel said to him, 'Gird yourself and put on your sandals.' And he did so. And he said to him, 'Wrap your cloak around you and follow me.' And he went out and continued to follow, and he did not know that what was being done by the angel was real, but thought he was seeing a vision. When they had passed the first and second guard, they came to the iron gate that leads into the city, which opened for them by itself; and they went out and went along one street, and immediately the angel departed from him. When Peter came to himself, he said, 'Now I know for sure that the Lord has sent forth His angel and rescued me from the hand of Herod and from all that the Jewish people were expecting.' And when he realized this, he went to the house of Mary, the mother of John who was also called Mark, where many were gathered together and were praying. When he knocked at the door of the gate, a servant-girl*

> named Rhoda came to answer. Then she recognized Peter's voice, because of her joy she did not open the gate, but ran in and announced that Peter was standing in front of the gate. They said to her, 'You are out of your mind!' But she kept insisting that it was so. They kept saying, 'It is his angel.'"

But Peter continued knocking; and when they had opened the door, they saw him and were amazed.

> "But motioning to them with his hand to be silent, he described to them how the Lord had led him out of the prison. And he said, 'Report these things to James and the brethren.' Then he left and went to another place. Now when day came, there was no small disturbance among the soldiers as to what could have become of Peter.

Peter described to those gathered in the church fellowship how the Lord (verse 17) had led him out of prison. One important part of this story is "*an angel of the Lord suddenly appeared in a light.*" In the Old Testament we do not find "angels of the Lord" appearing in the light. Jesus had ushered in the age of "light".

> **The Gospel brings God's truth into the world**

The Gospel brings the light of God to this world. The Gospel is the Truth of God, applicable to every life on earth, worshippers and clergy, rich and poor, redeemed and unredeemed. The Gospel is the revealed character, will, purpose and plan of the Holy God to His people for the purpose of fulfilling God's wishes and living a successful life.

Imagine again being chained to Peter. The brilliant light shines in a dark, smelly jail cell and the guards never notice it. Could it be the same "angel of the Lord" that awakened Peter put the guards in a deep trance?

Peter is instructed to dress and follow the angel. It is slightly humorous that Peter had to be struck by the angel to be awakened. Perhaps Peter rested in the peace of the Lord and was able to sleep while his life hung in uncertainty and false arrest. Maybe the same situation that caused the guards to be in a deep sleep also caused Peter to be in a deep sleep, thus the angel had to arouse Peter.

> *Jesus is the Light of the world. If we follow Him we will not walk in darkness*

The light of the Lord is important part of this discussion. We're focusing upon the "light of God". Light is the marvelous, life-giving gift of God Almighty to us His creation. Light is the illumination of His person, His will, His plan and His love for you and me. (Repeated for emphasis)

The Light of God is only revealed in the person of Jesus Christ. He said, "*I am the Light of the world; he who follows Me will not walk in the darkness but will have the Light of life.*" (John 8:12) Jesus, God with Us came to illuminate the lives of mankind and to show them Almighty God, The Father, Creator and Sustainer of life. Jesus alone is the Light!

Are you walking in the power of the Light? This idea will be addressed further in a later chapter. Meanwhile, let me suggest you ask this question of the Heavenly Father. Despite what we may think of ourselves, only He knows the truth. Wouldn't you rather have the testimony of the Holy Spirit about your walk than depend upon your own wisdom?

3 DARKNESS PREVENTS US FROM SEEING THE WAY

For our struggle is not against flesh and blood, but against the rulers, against the powers, against the world forces of this darkness, against the spiritual forces of wickedness in the heavenly places." (Ephesians 6:12)

Darkness is simply put, the absence of light. If you aren't sure about this truth, go into an enclosed room without windows or the influence of illumination. It's dark! The only way to maneuver around the room without injuring yourself is to turn a light on.

> ***Darkness is the absence of light***

During my early college years, I worked in a medical center hospital pharmacy. The pharmacy was located in the basement and had no windows. On one occasion I was working, and the electricity went out. When I say it was pitch dark, I mean I could not see my hand in front of my face. The only thing I could think of is not moving anything, my arms, legs or body. I had never seen such darkness.

When one lives in a metropolitan area there is never anything such as total darkness. No matter where you might be there is what's called light pollution or the radiation of light from some source no matter how far away.

My wife and I enjoy camping and mountains are our favorite. We camped once in Northwestern Montana near the Canadian border at Glacier National Park. If I were to say we were in the boonies that would be an understatement. There are no cities of any size nearby. There are so many tall mountains surrounding us that campsites were isolated. At our campsite we could see a sky that we do not normally see. The sky was alive with the lights of the heavens revealing themselves in a spectacular way. Despite the distant glow of the lights of the Heavens, we had to keep close-at-hand a dependable flashlight.

In the beginning of time there was nothing except God. As we see in Genesis 1:1-2, the earth was formless and darkness was over the surface. At this time God had not created the light of the heavens and so darkness ruled all of the time.

> *"In the beginning God created the heavens and the earth. The earth was formless and void, and darkness was over the surface."* (Genesis 1:1–2)

There are two references to light and darkness within Scriptures. Light represents either the absence of darkness or the righteousness of God. Darkness represents two different focuses: the absence of light (night) or evil.

The purpose of this chapter addresses darkness with the emphasis of evil. As a student of Scriptures I do not study darkness or Satan, but rather light and the Lord, God. Many years ago, I learned a lesson from the United States Treasury Department. Treasury agents never study counterfeit currency; they study only genuine U.S. treasury bills. They examine them endlessly until they know them so well that when a counterfeit bill does show up that doesn't match the real thing it catches their attention.

Studying the holiness, the character, the ways, purposes and plans of the Lord is studying the genuine. Then anything that doesn't match His revealed will within His Holy Word is a fake.

But in our present age there is so much confusion and uncertainty about the two that it bears a great need to examine the "darkness". We live in a time in which people are not thoroughly familiar with the genuine that it becomes necessary to dispel myths and reveal truths.

Before the beginning of time God had separated light from darkness. (Genesis 1:4) Darkness became known to God's people either as sin or as a curse. For example, when Moses approached Pharaoh about releasing his people, Pharaoh refused, again. So the Lord told Moses to stretch out his staff toward the sky and darkness filled the land. (Exodus 10:21-23)

> *"Then the* LORD *said to Moses, 'Stretch out your hand toward the sky, that there may be darkness over the land of Egypt, even a darkness which may be felt.' So Moses stretched out his hand toward the sky, and there was thick darkness in all the land of Egypt for three days. They did not see one another, nor did anyone rise from his place for three days, but all the sons of Israel had light in their dwellings."*

Can you imagine a complete and total blanket of darkness covering your home, your city, state or nation? What impact do you think that event would make on your emotions and sense of security? Would you be frightened? If it was this type of darkness all work of any kind stop. In today's economy it would probably mean economic disaster for businesses, industries and needed emergency services because they would have to shut down. It would most probably cause a mass hysteria like in a science-fiction movie.

Look at the effect this darkness would have on Egypt. *"They did not see one another, nor did anyone rise from his place for three days."* This event wasn't something that could be foretold by Egypt's astrologers, whom Pharaoh and cultures of that day greatly depended upon. This was a sudden event brought on by the Lord God, Creator of light, Himself, because Pharaoh would not heed God's demand to release the Hebrews. I believe it is important to note the fact that God created light and He alone can suspend it or control it.

One might be tempted to say, "Well this was a freak occurrence." Let me remind you of what the last phrase of verse 23 tell us, *"but all the sons of Israel had light in their dwellings."* If I were an Egyptian I think I would be deeply affected and possibly even terrified to know that one group of people had light and I didn't. Remember this was the cessation, or the absence, of all sunlight. The situation was as if the sun had merely quit shining only on the Egyptians. This fact alone would propel a nation into great distress.

Have you ever been in the Carlsbad Caverns in New Mexico? It's dark! Once you leave the cave entrance and journey into the bowels of the Earth, light grows dimmer and dimmer until there is no light. The only light within the caverns is the light brought in from the outside electric lines for safety. For some the fear of darkness is a real threat. The word for the fear of night is called Nyctophobia. The word is derived from Greek 'Nyctus 'meaning night or darkness and Phobos which means deep fear or dread.

Children are often afraid of the dark. Children and adults' imagination can go off the scale during times of darkness. Children can invent monsters living or hiding in their closets or under their beds at evening bedtime. Adults can be afraid to leave their home or to go into public places at night. Why? I suppose it is a fear of the unknown or a sense of the loss of security.

Most crime statistics indicate that the largest amount of crime is committed between sunset and sunrise. This is a time when it is dark. My understanding is that criminals do not want to be caught. Dark hours provide a more favorable time to commit crimes. One possible reason for this is they are in groups of friends, drinking and getting ideas of what would be fun. Whatever the reason darkness has its disadvantages for safety and security. Our local television news every morning reports the news from the previous night. I call it the "Knife and Gun Club Report."

> *In Scriptures darkness always refers to evil while light refers to righteousness.*

In Scriptures darkness always refers to evil while light refers to righteousness. There is a great deal of the New Testament addressing a person abiding or living (dwelling or remaining) in sin. Light and darkness can neither co-exist in the physical world nor can it in the spiritual world.

The word darkness (Greek – σκότος, pronounced skotos) is a noun. This noun can mean night darkness, darkened eyesight or blindness, but many times within Scriptures it refers to one's ignorance of God's ways or willfully knowing and failing to walk with those ways. This darkness refers to ungodliness and immorality, together with their consequential misery in hell.

This darkness is more dangerous than the mere absence of

illumination. This darkness brings the judgment of the Lord upon a person. For example, Exodus 10:21 – 23:

> *"The LORD said to Moses, 'Stretch out your hand toward the sky, that there may be darkness over the land of Egypt, even a darkness which may be felt.' So, Moses stretched out his hand toward the sky, and there was thick darkness in all the land of Egypt for three days. They did not see one another, nor did anyone rise from his place for three days, but all the sons of Israel had light in their dwellings."*

This was the ninth judgment of God upon Egypt. I do not claim to be a Bible scholar but in my personal study of Scriptures the "plagues" in Exodus were actuality judgments. They are judgments because they are the human results of outright denial of Who God is and His plainly stated purpose and desires. Believers know that God will judge the world in the end of time, but the judgment of the Lord can be given and has been given before Jesus' final return in the book of Revelation.

There are many references in the New Testament to the judgment of the Lord. In 1 Thessalonians 5:5 the Apostle Paul refers to this specific day as the *"day of the Lord"*. This phrase is within several passages, such as: 1 Corinthians 1:8 and 5:5. In 2 Peter 2:9 it is called "the day of judgment".

Darkness is an expression of the presence of the ruler of this world, Satan. In John 16:11, Satan is called the "prince (ruler) of this world." The Word of God, not me, defines Satan the ruler of darkness or evil. Throughout the Scriptures Satan has had many different names. Each name of Satan is one of opposition to God, His purposes, His plans and His holiness. According to Revel's Bible dictionary, the New Testament, Satan is mentioned 36 times as diabolos (slanderer). In addition, there are other descriptive names of Satan throughout the New Testament: (pg. 896)

- Accuser of our brothers (Revelation 12:10)
- That ancient serpent (Revelation 12:9)
- Satan is the ruler of darkness Abaddon and Appollyon (destroyer- Revelation 9:11)
- Beelzebub (Matthew 12:24)
- Belial (2 Corinthians 6:15)
- Your enemy (1 Peter 5:8)
- The evil one (Matthew 13:19)
- The father of lies (John 8:44)
- The god of this age (2 Corinthians 4:4)
- The great dragon (Revelation 12:9)
- A murderer (John 8:44)
- The one who leads the whole world astray (Revelation 12:9)
- Prince of this world (John 12:31)
- Ruler of the kingdom of the air (Ephesians 2:2)
- The spirit at work in those who are disobedient (Ephesians 2:2)
- The tempter (Matthew 4:3)

> *Satan is the ruler of darkness*

The New Testament develops the idea of Satan as the "anti-Christ" because he works diligently to oppose the person and the work of Christ. This is once again a person, the person of Satan, the god of his age. This phrase was coined by John and found in his letters (1 John 2:18; 22; 4:3; and 2 John 2:7)

Too often we place the antichrist at the end of time in which the great battle for eternity between Satan and Jesus occurs followed by the end of times. While there will be "the anti-Christ" be warned these antichrists are already with us on earth and have been around especially described since the resurrection and ascension of Jesus. John wrote:

> *"Children, it is the last hour; and just as you heard that antichrist is coming, even now many antichrists have appeared; from this we know that it is the last hour."* (1 John 2:18)

"Who is the liar but the one who denies that Jesus is the Christ? This is the antichrist, the one who denies the Father and the Son." (1 John 2:22)

"By this you know the Spirit of God: every spirit that confesses that Jesus Christ has come in the flesh is from God; and every spirit that does not confess Jesus is not from God; this is the spirit of the antichrist, of which you have heard that it is coming, and now it is already in the world." (1 John 4:2–3)

"For many deceivers have gone out into the world, those who do not acknowledge Jesus Christ as coming in the flesh. This is the deceiver and the antichrist." (2 John 7)

> **Satan, has been around since the beginning of time**
>
> **(Genesis 3:1-14)**

The Epistle of John was written in the first century. Almost from the beginning of the Christian time, there has been someone to oppose the message, the ministry and the influence of Jesus upon a culture and a way of life. The ruler of darkness, Satan, has been around since the beginning of time (Genesis 3:1-14), not just a futuristic character of Revelation. In addition, he is not a figment of someone's imagination, as many of the people of the modern world today believes. He is real and he is a real threat, but not to fear – John wrote, *"You are from God, little children, and have overcome them (reference to the antichrist); because greater is He who is in you than he who is in the world."* (1 John 4:4)

Darkness and evil have always been around from the beginning of time until the end of time when the final battle is won and Satan is cast into the eternal prison. Satan is here to distract us, trip us and derail us, his power and his presence are limited. He cannot be everywhere (omnipresent) as God is. Satan is not omnipotent (all powerful) as God is. The deceiver is not all-knowing (omniscient) as our Heavenly Father.

Should you think Satan is "all powerful" and can do anything, you need to look at the book of Job.

> *"Now there was a day when the sons of God came to present themselves before the LORD, and Satan also came among them. The LORD said to Satan, 'From where do you come?' Then Satan answered the LORD and said, 'From roaming about on the earth and walking around on it. The LORD said to Satan, 'Have you considered My servant Job? For there is no one like him on the earth, a blameless and upright man, fearing God and turning away from evil. Then Satan answered the LORD, 'Does Job fear God for nothing? Have You not made a hedge about him and his house and all that he has, on every side? You have blessed the work of his hands, and his possessions have increased in the land. But put forth Your hand now and touch all that he has; he will surely curse You to Your face.' Then the LORD said to Satan, 'Behold, all that he has is in your power, only do not put forth your hand on him.' So Satan departed from the presence of the LORD."* (Job 1:6-12)

Notice verse 6 where Satan comes before the Lord. The phrase *"sons of God came to present themselves before the LORD"* is understood to indicate the angels of Heaven were standing in the presence of the Lord. There is a thought that the angels were giving an account of their ministry to the faithful of God and to possibly receive future instructions. Whatever the meeting was about, Satan thrust himself into this assembly, probably to distract and disturb the holy gathering.

While in the presence of the Holy One, (verse 7) God asked Satan where he came from he responded, *"From roaming about on the earth and walking around on it."* What an answer responding to Lord Almighty! Satan's answer has a strong hint of bitterness and animosity towards The Creator and God of the universe. Satan still had access to Heaven, but the point here is Satan plainly shows how he falsely accuses the faithful of not being worthy of God's love and attention.

Satan's answer indicates what he does, "roams and walks the earth." In Peter's first epistle (1 Peter 5:8) he warned the church, *"Be of sober spirit, be on the alert. Your adversary, the devil, prowls around like a roaring lion, seeking someone to devour."*

Satan is complaining about being forced to walk on earth while God enjoys the presence of Heaven. Satan's response draws a question from God. The LORD said to Satan, *"Have you considered My servant Job? For there is no one like him on the earth, a blameless and upright man, fearing God and turning away from evil."* (Verse 8)

If you were raised with other siblings you may remember how your parents might have said, "Look at the way your brother or sister behaves (acts, manners, grades and dresses). This is a parental way of using one child's life as an example of how another child should live. You could say the parent is using a living example to show someone else a desired behavior. God's question to Satan has that tone, too. While Satan was complaining. Can you imagine God saying, "Hey, look at Job, there's no one like him." God was definitely pointing out the exceptional life Job was living.

What Satan said next was probably his attempt to lure Mighty God into proving Job's standing. *Satan said, "Does Job fear God for nothing? Have You not made a hedge about him and his house and all that he has, on every side? You have blessed the work of his hands, and his possessions have increased in the land. 'But put forth Your hand now and touch all that he has; he will surely curse You to Your face.'"* (Job 1:9-11)

Job's response to Satan's affliction shows how he blesses the Lord not for what He does for Job, but for Who God is.

> *"He said, 'Naked I came from my mother's womb, and naked I shall return there. The LORD gave and the LORD has taken away. Blessed be the name of the LORD.' Through all this Job did not sin nor did he blame God".* (Job 1:21-22)

Shouldn't this be every child of God's response?'

The point of this long discussion is to show you that while God's power is unmeasurable and unlimited Satan's power has definite limits. God set the limit by telling Satan that he can touch everything surrounding Job but his life. *"Then the LORD said to Satan, '"Behold, all that he has is in your power, only do not put forth your hand on him.' So Satan departed from the presence of the LORD.'"* (Job 1:12)

Both Satan and God had confidence. Satan believed that Job's faithfulness was because God did everything for him and the moment he lost it all, he would denounce God. Yet, God had confidence in Job because of Job's unwavering faithful, loving character. There are many followers of Christ who experience such persecution. They have a choice to renounce Jesus or die. They die! This is the biblical idea of following or believing Jesus.

We have seen the darkness of "the deceiver" on earth. Seemingly the most famous Twentieth Century example of a person deeply influenced by Satan was Adolph Hitler. The German dictator was either directly or indirectly responsible for human carnage in the millions. He brought immeasurable suffering to the entire world through his "unholy" desire for power, prestige and position.

We have also witnessed many others here in America, too. In the late Twentieth Century men such as: Charles Manson, Jim Jones, Ted Bundy, John Wayne Gacy, and Jeffrey Dahmer all gave rise to indescribable atrocities. These men each shocked the American society as their crimes became apparent. These and many more demonstrated a complete lack of any moral compass much less the Spirit of the Living God.

Do you ever watch the local news? Our city's news stations wake up the city with the usual traffic and weather reports, but as an added treat they give what I call the "Knife and Gun Club Report" of all the murders that happened the night before. I personally have never understood why they do this unless it to sensationalize the news and have something to do because their reports seem to have no public service announcement value. But if you've ever watched the local news you will understand about darkness and its consequences upon the people committing the crimes and their victims.

Darkness is an indication of the lack of presence of the Lord God in the culture and individual lives and has several demonstrations. Darkness is definitely manifested in monstrous crimes but is also shown in one's attitude toward our Heavenly Father, His servants and children. We presently live in a "post-church or post-Christian era in which people have little to no interest in spiritual matters. We have contained in the New Testament Scriptures prophecies about the times we live. The Apostle Paul wrote to young Pastor Timothy in the first century (approximately 64/65 A.D.):

> *Darkness indicates a lack of God's presence*

> *"But realize this, that in the last days difficult times will come. For men will be lovers of self, lovers of money, boastful, arrogant, revilers, disobedient to parents, ungrateful, unholy, unloving, irreconcilable, malicious gossips, without self-control, brutal, haters of good, treacherous, reckless, conceited, lovers of pleasure rather than lovers of God, holding to a form of godliness, although they have denied its power; Avoid such men as these. For among them are those who enter into households and captivate weak women weighed down with sins, led on by various impulses, always learning and never able to come to the knowledge of the truth. Just as Jannes and Jambres opposed Moses, so these men also oppose the truth, men of depraved mind, rejected in regard to the faith."* (2 Timothy 3:1–9)

The Apostle Peter wrote his epistle, or letter, in approximately 64 - 65 A.D. Peter would prophecy two thousand years in the future about spiritual attitudes of our day. He said,

> *"Know this first of all, that in the last days mockers will come with their mocking, following after their own lusts, and saying, 'Where is the promise of His coming? For ever since the fathers fell asleep, all continues just as it was from the beginning of creation.'"* (2 Peter 3:3–4)

The fact that several of God's men wrote about the time when darkness would increase over the lands, should not surprise anyone. God has used prophecies throughout time to warn and prepare His people about the experiences we will face and His instructions to them. God is a timeless God. He exists outside of time, which is difficult for us to understand. Before the first second hand tick of the clock, God existed. Beyond the last second of time following the apocalypse, God will exist. He is eternal, without beginning or end. The Mighty God can, unlike us, see from eternity past to eternity future. That is one reason why we should trust Him with our lives today and our souls for all eternity.

Here's a point that is tough for most people to wrap their understanding. We can only see what's happening right this moment. We are not able to see our future, yet God can. Time does not restrict the Lord God who created everything! This fact gives rise to the understanding that when Jehovah God wants to prepare His children, He will inspire someone to make known His truths. That is precisely what the Lord God did with these men, such as: Paul, Peter, John and people throughout the past two millennia. Many of the Old Testament books are prophecies. They contain future events and warnings, which by the way have come true or been fulfilled. Many of these prophecies are documented in history, such as the fall of the Temple in Jerusalem, just to mention one.

Jesus made many prophecies of which many biblical scholars still study. The ultimate prophecy God made to John in the New Testament book of Revelation. The child of God should understand or remember that prophecy is two-fold: the foretelling of future events and forth-telling of God's truth or preaching today.

The fact that people of the Twenty-first century have God's timeless Word in Scriptures to warn us should also prepare us for our spiritual function to warn others of their eternal choices through our ministry of evangelism. But the Prince of Darkness has convinced many leaders today and many in the pews that we are in danger if we leave the monastery walls of the church and we should stay with our own kind, not venture out into the world and risk our lives by telling anyone about the marvelous grace we have through Jesus, the Son of God. I say, in ancient Babylonian, "hog wash!"

Do you fear the world more than you trust God to take care of you? I only fear one thing – disappointing my Heavenly Father, Almighty God!

In the preceding four verses John wrote this,

> *"In the beginning was the Word, and the Word was with God, and the Word was God. He was in the beginning with God. All things came into being through Him, and apart from Him nothing came into being that has come into being. In Him was life, and the life was the Light of men."* John 1:1-4)

This passage gives the reader a great deal of insight into the deity of Jesus. Let me try to keep it simple. Our English word, "Word" comes from a Greek word "logos". This word actually means, in the spiritual world, the revelation of God. God spoke, that's the Word. God instructed the prophets to record His Word. Verses 1-4 give us great theological truths:

1. In the beginning there was the Word. (God) This is also an expression of the equality of Jesus with the person of God and their co-existence.

2. By the hand of God, the Son, all creation came to be.

3. God, the Son, contained life, was life and today is life. An understanding that life only exist in and through the Person of Jesus because He was responsible for creation

4. "In Him was life and the life was the Light of Men." All that is within us that is of value: knowledge, integrity, intelligent, willing subjection to God, love of Him and to their fellow creatures, wisdom, purity, holy joy, rational happiness come from the spring of Jesus.

The person of Jesus brings meaning to and value of the individual through a life committed to Him through salvation. We need Jesus to fill our empty, dark person with Himself. Without the Light of

God through Jesus Christ, we walk in darkness and life has no meaning. All of the activities, all of our material goods and our wealth means nothing because they do not give us meaning and all of this is just a short answer to our real needs – **to walk in the light**.

> *Darkness is living a continuous lifestyle of disobedience to God*

Darkness is an idea of living or walking continuously in a lifestyle of sin or disobedience to God. The Gospel of John gives us great detail about walking in darkness compared to walking in the light. The first truth regarding walking in darkness is found in John 1:5. John wrote, *"The Light shines in the darkness, and the darkness did not comprehend it."*

Once I was driving in Southeast Louisiana and I saw the traffic light change from green to red and simply without thought drove through it. On the opposite side of the intersection sat a Louisiana State Trooper. Immediately she pulled me over and asked why I ran that light. I told her the absolute truth, "I saw it but for some reason my mind was somewhere else and I kept on driving." The humor is that she did not give me a ticket.

Living or continuing to live in sin is the universal disease afflicting all of mankind. This disease is the most catastrophic and preventable disease on earth. Modern medicine has cured Polio and many different infectious diseases through inoculations and cleanliness. However, there is only one available cure for sin. Jesus!

We were all born with the infection of sin. We were born into sin through Adam and Eve. Sin is in our DNA. Scientists are still searching for this gene and one day will probably find it. But in the meantime every human being on earth must struggle through this deadly disease.

I am sure you might be tempted to say, "Not me! I'm forgiven. Or you might be tempted to think you have never sinned or since you became a Christian you no longer are tempted to sin or cross over into its bowels. Let me give you a rest from your wrestling with this thought.

> *"All have sinned"* (Romans 3:23)

> *"If we say that we have no sin, we are deceiving ourselves and the truth is not in us. If we confess our sins, He is faithful and righteous to forgive us our sins and to cleanse us from all unrighteousness. If we say that we have not sinned, we make Him a liar and His word is not in us."* (1 John 1:8–10)

The Apostle John calls our attention to three truths here:

1. Only a deceived mind can say, "I have no sin." The deception comes from Satan himself trying to convince you, "You're o.k." when you aren't.

2. If we refuse to accept the fact we have sin then the "truth is not in us." Truth is not a concept, it is a person. His name is Jesus. Upon the ascension of Jesus every believer was given the Holy Spirit at Pentecost. The Holy Spirit is God. He comes to remind us of what He taught through His Son, Jesus, to convict us of sin, and to unify us into one body. So, if we are redeemed then we are sensitive to the leading of the Holy Spirit whom will convict us when we sin.

3. Third, should we say, "I have not sinned," then we make God out to be a liar when His Word tells us we are all sinners.

The Holy Spirit is like a warning light on an auto engine. He warns us before we sin so that we might not sin. Afterward the Holy Spirit convicts us if we have sinned. We have all had warning lights activate that warn us of low gas or an engine problem. Duh! Why do we ignore them? A lot of times our mind is somewhere else, or we say to ourselves, "I'll get to it later." But, don't we sometimes ignore the warning?

John wrote in verse 5, *"The Light shines in the darkness, and the darkness did not comprehend it."* In our dark and fallen world of sin we sit in darkness without the ability to find the way either of truth or of holiness. In this darkness and consequent intellectual and moral obscurity "the Light of the Word" shines but despite the brightness of the revealed will of God, we are not able to see it, comprehend it or apply it to our lives unless we have been redeemed and given the Holy Spirit. We are instructed that *"the god of this world has blinded the minds of the unbelieving so that they might not see the light of the gospel of the glory of Christ, who is the image of God."* (2 Corinthians 4:4) We have eyes, but cannot see and ears but cannot hear the message of God. We cannot understand it because Satan has numbed us to the voice of God.

Darkness is the idea of the judgements of the Lord. Judgment is a condemnation or in the case of a criminal trial a rendering of a legal decision. In some countries this is done entirely by a judge, but in our nation, it is most often done by a jury.

A trial presents one's proof or evidence to support the charge of guilt. The defense team attempts to discredit the evidence and support a defense strategy to get their client off with a "not guilty". Once both arguments are completed the judge turns to the jury for a final verdict. Their job is to take the evidence, consider whether the person is actually guilty or not and then render their findings with a "guilty or not guilty".

The idea of judgment seems to be strained the days. One camp says, "God wouldn't judge me and send me to hell." They're right. God doesn't send us to hell, we send ourselves by our choices to ignore God's Word and do whatever it is that pleases "me". The other camp says, "God doesn't judge the Christian because we've been forgiven on Calvary's cross." Well, this is partially true and partially untrue.

> *"For we must all appear before the judgment seat of Christ that each one may receive what is due him for the things done while in the body, whether good or bad."* (2 Corinthians 5:10, NIV)

Forgiveness for all sin has been made available through the death, burial and resurrection of the Lord, Jesus Christ, but there's one thing we invariably leave out – repentance. Repentance is not a feeling or words we may say, repentance is an action. Repentance is a turning away from that sin, whether a lifestyle of a reoccurring occurrence. Forgiveness, even for the Christian is achieved through repentance.

In John 8 the story is told of a woman caught in adultery. She was brought out to be stoned, which was the usual and customary punishment for this sin in Jesus' day. As Jesus doodled in the sand her accusers began to leave. He asked her, *"Woman, where are they? Did no one condemn you?" She said, "No one, Lord." And Jesus said, "I do not condemn you, either. Go. From now on sin no more."* (John 8:10–11)

The woman's accusers, the Pharisees brought this woman to Jesus as a test. If Jesus had condemned her, he would be contradicting everything He had been teaching and all that He stood for. If Jesus dismissed her sin he would be guilty of heresy. No one knows what Jesus was writing in the sand with His finger, but when he turned to the woman and asked, "Where are your accusers," the answer was simple – they are no longer here condemning you for sin and neither do I. Then she received an answer that we should all pay serious attention, "Go and sin no more!" The Pharisees argument faded away because Jesus neither dismissed her sin or condemned her.

Repentance is often tough to do for us all. Changing appears to be something our bodies do with aging, but we do not like changing our minds to be able to change our lifestyles. Let me give you my thinking. Take someone who has drank alcohol or even taken prescription drugs for a long time, it is very difficult to put them aside. Another example is a person who lives in bitterness at something or someone. Forgiveness or settlement of that anger is difficult to overcome. I am sure you can think of your own examples that you have experienced through your life or witnessed in others. The point is this – unless we repent of our sin, forgiveness is unavailable. Let me share a few verses:

> *"From that time Jesus began to preach and say, 'Repent, for the kingdom of heaven is at hand.'"* (Matthew 4:17)

> *"Then He began to denounce the cities in which most of His miracles were done, because they did not repent. Woe to you, Chorazin! Woe to you, Bethsaida! For if the miracles had occurred in Tyre and Sidon which occurred in you, they would have repented long ago in sackcloth and ashes. Nevertheless, I say to you, it will be more tolerable for Tyre and Sidon in the day of judgment than for you."* (Matthew 11:20–22)

> *Jesus sent His twelve disciples out into the countryside to proclaim the Good News and we are told, "They went out and preached that men should repent."* (Mark 6:12)

> *"For all have sinned and fallen short of the glory of God."* (Romans 3:23)

> *"I tell you, no, but unless you repent, you will all likewise perish".* (Luke 13:3)

> *"For the wages of sin is death,"* (Romans 6:23)

> *"The Lord is not slow about His promise, as some count slowness, but is patient toward you, not wishing for any to perish but for all to come to repentance."* (2 Peter 3:9)

> *"But the free gift of God is eternal life in Christ Jesus our Lord."* (Romans 6:23b)

God is serious about sin (walking in darkness) but He has made a way to be released from the bondage of sin. He has given us a gift (Romans 6:23b) and that gift's name is Jesus. He came to bear the penalty for our sin even though He was guiltless. Jesus became our substitutionary sacrifice. No one can get around repentance from our sin. It is possible through and only by the Lord Jesus.

Let me explain it this way. A man is seen by many witnesses shooting and killing a person. He is tried in a court of law and found guilty. The judge imposes the death penalty for your crime and the penalty is death. (Romans 6:23) But someone else offers to pay our penalty by giving their life as a substitution for you. This is precisely what Jesus did. Every human ever born was born into sin and has a need to be reconciled or our sin issue settle with God. All of this sounds pretty unbelievable, but that's the level of love God has for you, to allow His own Son, Jesus to die on the cross so that you and I might be saved.

I have sinned against God and deserve to die on the cross. You have sinned against God and deserved to die on that cross. Every human being ever born, except Jesus, has sinned against God and deserve to die, but Jesus stepped in and paid our sin debt.

I want you to consider what is in this chapter and ask the Lord God, "Am I walking in darkness?" Do not depend upon your own wisdom or insight into this matter; it is a spiritual matter that only the Living God can answer through the Holy Spirit. Let me invite you to simply pray like this,

> "Almighty God, am I walking blindly in darkness? Speak to me, I await Your answer and make it clear and plain that I may truly understand. If I am walking in darkness, please give me the direction, since I cannot see the way or know the way and give me Your strength to enable me to repent. Amen."

The way is Jesus.

> *"Jesus said to him, 'I am the way, and the truth, and the life; no one comes to the Father but through Me.'"* (John 14:6)

Would you be willing to go to the Way, the Truth and the Life? In Jesus one can walk in the Light of God and release from walking in darkness and sin. One can discover the peace and joy of walking in the Eternal Light.

> *"And the book of the prophet Isaiah was handed to Him. And He opened the book and found the place where it was written, 'The Spirit of the Lord is upon Me, Because He anointed Me to preach the gospel to the poor. He has sent Me to proclaim release to the captives, and recovery of sight to the blind, to set free those who are oppressed, to proclaim the favorable year of the Lord. And He closed the book, gave it back to the attendant and sat down; and the eyes of all in the synagogue were fixed on Him. And He began to say to them, "Today this Scripture has been fulfilled in your hearing."* (Luke 4:17–21)

Jesus came with the only keys to the handcuffs which bind you to Satan. (verse 18) Can you think of one good reason why you would not want to be freed from your sin and its penalty?

> **Jesus came with the only keys to the handcuffs which bind you to Satan**

In verse 21 Jesus identified that the prophecy of Isaiah, in which He was reading had been fulfilled. This prophecy was made in the 7th Century B.C. about the long-expected Messiah. The proclamation of the Gospel message would achieve these miraculous events (verses 18-19) and establish a great celebration in the heart of the Gospel message hearers.

You see, Jesus is talking about the bondage to sin. When one is freed from that enslavement and its consequence, one is truly freed! The "favorable year of the Lord" refers to the Jewish custom of The Year of Jubilee recorded in Leviticus 25:10

> *"You shall thus consecrate the fiftieth year and proclaim a release through the land to all its inhabitants. It shall be a jubilee for you, and each of you shall return to his own property, and each of you shall return to his family."*

Every 7 years was known as a "Sabbatical year" for the nation. The land was allowed to rest, a time when all slaves were set free and returned to their families and all debts were cancelled. The Sabbatical year was a time in which the people's burdens were eliminated. This was a time in which the groans of the suffering of humanity under the names of poverty, broken-heartedness, bondage, blindness, when the state of individual bruised (or crushed) feelings were addressed by God Himself and relief was given relief.

Humanity, walking in darkness is in a state of constantly being crushed by the weight of each individual's sin. People are desperately attempting to get from under this weight and seek just about any method for relief. Jesus said in the Luke 4:17-21 that He had come to do precisely that. You may have seen an old movie where a person owed a huge debt to another person and he was constantly badgered, harassed and threatened if the debt wasn't settled. Imagine having someone unrelated to you stepping in and paying that debt on your behalf. Would you feel an enormous weight lifted? Would you be grateful?

This is exactly what Jesus did on the cross. He took the sins of humanity upon His shoulders and paid the debt we could not pay – death for a debt He did not owe. Think of the love displayed by Jesus for you.

Stepping out of the darkness into the Light should be a tremendous relief and a deep celebration. I hope it is for you.

Meanwhile there is another group that neither walks in the light nor the darkness. They walk in both. In chapter 4 I call them "Shadow Walkers".

4 WALKING IN THE SHADOWS IS COSTLY

I know your deeds, that you are neither cold nor hot; I wish that you were cold or hot. So, because you are lukewarm, and neither hot nor cold, I will spit you out of My mouth." (Revelation 3:15–16)

Many years ago, I witness one of the most phenomenal natural occurrences of my life. It was nearly noon and scientist had predicted a solar eclipse. They gave all of the warnings and told us where it would be the strongest and went on and on.

I walked out on the sidewalk in front of work, facing nearly south, and watched the effects upon the ground and buildings. As the eclipse occurred the normal daylight turned a kind of pumpkin orange. The normal sunlight for noon was highly subdued. I felt as though I was on the show "Star Trek" and I was standing on Vulcan or some weird planet. Truthfully, it was a little frightening and definitely strange because I was neither walking in the light of the sun nor in the darkness of night – somewhere between.

The majority of Christians world-wide walk in the faithfulness of God's life. This group tries with great effort to be faithful and obedient to the Lord. Many of these people have little to nothing in life and depend upon the mercy and grace of the Lord Jesus. They realize they may be in bondage to an evil war lord or dictator or suppressed freedom. In these situations, they are not much more than a number or an animal. What they lack is respect, love and the ability to do as they choose. These faithful followers of Jesus may be surrounded by those who hate God and hate even more those who are His children. This group walks in the light surrounded by darkness.

Then there is a large portion of people who call themselves Christian but cannot comprehend a deep commitment to Christ. Involvement in the Kingdom's work is something they have little to no interest. Some are members of a local church and attend regularly while other will occasionally attend; the thought of sinking their life into the fellowship of believers and actively working to see others come to the saving knowledge of Jesus Christ is just not their thing. These folks live for themselves and no one else.

Please do not mistake the intent of this chapter. Instantly, one might think I am talking about sinless perfection in our lives here on earth. The New Testament indicates that we all have sinned and fallen short of the glory of God. (Romans 3:23) Sinless perfection is only for the person who has surrendered their lives to Jesus in salvation and they have reached Heaven. That is the time in which God's children are remade into the image of Jesus, which had no sin on earth. (2 Corinthians 5:21) In our walk on earth we are only striving to be as close to sin-free as possible. Let me show you what the New Testament says about this problem.

> *"My dear children, I write this to you so that you will not sin. But if anybody does sin, we have one who speaks to the Father in our defense — Jesus Christ, the Righteous One. He is the atoning sacrifice for our sins, and not only for ours but also for the sins of the whole world."* (1John 2:1-2)

> **A shadow walker is one attempting to walk in the light of Christ and the darkness of this world at the same time**

Some people simply do not usually give much effort to walking in the light. Jesus addressed this issue in what I'm calling "Shadow Walkers." A shadow walker is one attempting to walk in the light of Christ and the darkness of this at the same time. Some would call these "fence straddlers". These people that want what is on both sides, this temporary world with the benefits of eternality in heaven.

Throughout the years of pastoring, I have noticed those walking in darkness, those walking in the light and those trying to walk in both or the shadows. These poor souls never discover the power of the transforming power of the Lord. They seem to be extremely happy with spiritual mediocrity. Their lives are lived in the twilight just prior to sunrise or just before night fall. They are neither hot nor cold but lukewarm. Jesus said, *"I know your deeds, that you are neither cold nor hot; I wish that you were cold or hot. So, because you are lukewarm, and neither hot nor cold, I will spit you out of My mouth."* (Revelation 3:15–16)

During my youth, many of my friends loved to drink beer. I sipped it, but never really liked it because of its taste. My friends would race to drink the beer before it became slightly warm. Once it turned from ice-cold to nearing room temperature, they would discard the remainder of the bottle and get another "cold one". I would sip mine very slowly and allow it to get to the temperature of which they threw theirs away. Once my beer warmed up, I would drink it. My friends did not like lukewarm beer!

Try another analogy. Many people enjoy cold coffee. Still a larger portion of the society prefers hot coffee. Once coffee cools off they, too, will discard that cup and get a refill of hot coffee. This group of people do not like lukewarm coffee. Me, I wait until my coffee cools down before I drink it.

Go back to Revelation 3:15–16 where Jesus said, "I wish that you were cold or hot. So, because you are lukewarm, and neither hot nor cold, I will spit you out of My mouth." Doesn't this fit with the idea of our favorite hot or cold beverage. We have a favorite range of temperature for the beverage we drink, the food we eat or the room in which we sleep. We make adjustments in the room temperature of strive to get the food and drink that matches our temperature liking.

Jesus relates the idea of faithfulness to the consumption of food or drink. Ideally, we want food and drink served at a correct temperature. Jesus has a standard too. He relates His standard of faithfulness to something people of His day and ours will understand. If a person is not committed to Christ, they give Him a bad taste and is completely unsatisfying, as a servant of God.

Shadow walkers aren't evil people, like the ones in darkness. They are usually good natured, perhaps generous and especially fun loving. Some of the shadow walkers may have been baptized, on the church's membership role and even in Sunday school, but if they are not walking in the light, they are either walking in darkness or the shadows. These fence straddlers try to please everyone at the same time, but many times end up displeasing the One most important person, God.

I ran across a pastor's website recently that shows this point. Joe McKeever (joemckeever.com) posted a story to his ministry website that is revealing and sad. He has given me permission to use story in the book. It reads:

When a pastor gets called to an ignorant church

Posted on May 23, 2013 by Joe McKeever

"But grow in the grace and knowledge of our Lord and Savior Jesus Christ" (II Peter 3:18).

"There is enough ignorance in this county to ignorantize the whole country."

"What happens when a pastor gets called to a church like that?" A church where the members and leaders alike do not know the Word of God and have no idea of how things should be done (what Paul called "how one ought to conduct himself in the household of God"–I Timothy 3:15), or why it all matters.

A church that exists to condemn sin and sinners, that knows only slivers of Scripture, that sees ministers as slaves of the whims of the congregation, and that is ready to reject as a liberal any minister who wants the church to feed the hungry in the community, take a stand for justice, or invite in the minority neighbors.

We wish we could say such congregations are few and rare, but they aren't. Veteran preachers have stories of those churches, tales of run-ins with those leaders, and scars from the battles they have waged to set matters right.

One pastor told the group of ministers meeting in his fellowship hall, "This building is actually owned by a member of the KKK. We rent it from him." The rest of us were naive and thought the Ku Klux Klan had died out ages ago. Here they were living among us in our own southern town.

One lady visible in church leadership told her pastor, "I don't know what the Bible says but I know what I believe."

Another church allowed a deacon and a woman Sunday School teacher to live together as husband and wife but without being married. The head deacon admitted the rest of them were too cowardly to confront the outspoken couple. When the new pastor tried to deal with it, the couple turned on him and slandered him in the community. Finding himself isolated with no support from the congregation, he resigned and moved away.

It is not true that such churches know nothing of the Bible. They know snippets of it, depending on what previous pastors majored on. Some went to seed on prophecy (a typical sermon dealt with the antichrist or the beast of Revelation) or salvation (every sermon was "get saved now!") or works (the pastor defined the proper length of women's hemlines and the amount of makeup they were allowed, the proper raising of children, and such)."

These stories hit close to home and every account I have heard from other pastors are just as troubling and revealing as these stories. Throughout the years the Lord has had me re-energizing or revitalizing churches. Most, but not all, people in these churches were good, Godly people. But I have heard on more than one occasion men who were considered leaders in the church say, "I would rather make Jesus mad than my neighbor."

The price of following Jesus is costly. What does one hope to gain by having one foot in the world and one foot in the Kingdom? Actually, one cannot put one foot in the world and one foot in the Kingdom, but this is an illustration of a point of commitment. This would be as if you or I were married to two different spouses at the same time. Where's commitment? Where's faithfulness? Most people I know or have known would not tolerate another spouse sharing their spouse's

> *The price of following Jesus is costly*

affection and time. There are two possible sounds the two-timing spouse may hear: "Get out of here," followed by something thrown or a gun fire. Just kidding."

The walking in two worlds could mean two things. First, one is not completely convinced in the reality of Jesus and His teachings. But just in case He is real, I will become one of His followers. They may say, "But I will keep myself at a distance." Some call this attitude fire insurance. I am prepared just in case He is real.

> *"Then Jesus said to His disciples, 'If anyone wishes to come after Me, he must deny himself, and take up his cross and follow Me. For whoever wishes to save his life will lose it; but whoever loses his life for My sake will find it. For what will it profit a man if he gains the whole world and forfeits his soul? Or what will a man give in exchange for his soul?' 'For the Son of Man is going to come in the glory of His Father with His angels, and WILL THEN REPAY EVERY MAN ACCORDING TO HIS DEEDS.'"* (Matthew 16:24–27)

Our famous 16th President of the United States, Abraham Lincoln once said, "You can please some of the people some of the time, all of the people some of the time, some of the people all of the time, but you can never please all of the people all of the time."

> *Every person has a great need to be transformed from the "dark side" to the "light side" without stopping in the shadows.*

Previously in chapter 1, I mentioned Jesus' transformation when He appeared to have become as bright as a light. This event, as previously stated, was witnessed with astonishment by three of the disciples. God, the Father expects everyone who follows His Son, Jesus to be transformed into the image of Jesus.

"Therefore, I urge you, brethren, by the mercies of God, to present your bodies a living and holy sacrifice, acceptable to God, which is your spiritual service of worship. And do not be conformed to this world, but be transformed by the renewing of your mind, so that you may prove what the will

> *of God is, that which is good and acceptable and perfect."* (Romans 12:1–2)

Romans 12:1-2 gives you and I a high expectation of what God expects of every person that has been born again or redeemed. Many people focus on the outward appearance but here we see that God focuses on the inward person. We may have had a physical transformation by the way we dress but has our hearts and minds changed? This, as indicated in the verse, one is transformed by the renewing or making new our minds or thoughts and wishes.

Our thoughts indicate our character. Yet, our thoughts drive our actions. If a person is preoccupied on the ways of the world, actions will soon match our thoughts which are a reflection of our character. But, God expects our minds to be made new, too. What we once thought of before salvation should be completely different after salvation. Instead of focusing on the here and now or what I want, we begin focusing upon how can I make the lives of other better? How can I can minister to another person? How can I bless God today? Is my prayer life filled with "me" or "Him"?

There are so many adjustments in our thinking that has to take place that we must constantly seek God's answers through His Holy Spirit and allow Him to guide us in His truth. Each one of us is incapable of achieving the transformed mind in our own power. It is only done by the power of Almighty God through His Son, Jesus.

Every person has a great need to be transformed from the "dark side" to the "light side" without stopping in the shadows. Completing this process requires a total make-over or transformation. We're talking about making lead into gold (as alchemist once tried). This transformation is the goal of our redemption, as written in Romans 8:29, *"For those whom He foreknew, He also predestined to become conformed to the image of His Son, so that He would be the firstborn among many brethren;"*

So many products are advertised todays as "changing your life." These products may make some things easier, but nothing or anyone can change your life unless you first are open to the idea. Jesus will never invade your life and force you to change. He will lead you, but you must be willing to be led and be an open vessel for Him to begin the transformation process.

Too many brides-to-be go into marriage saying, "I'm going to change my husband." Love makes us do some crazy things and this is crazy to think about or try. There again, only Jesus can change a person and it may take a life time. In many years of counseling with people in our church, it never fails someone will come to me wanting to know why they've failed to change their husband. Aren't you glad you don't have the ability to change someone else? What we might do may be worse than what we had. But, if Jesus transforms both people into His image – now think of what are the possibilities?

The shadow walker, for some reason, is not able to proceed through the process of a spiritual transformation. They become like some horrific experiment on a 1950's science fiction movie, like the fly, caught between two conflicting states of existence. In one version of the movie "The Fly" the person became neither human nor insect, but parts of both. For the shadow walker they may consciously desire to walk in the light of God but by the choices they make they walk in darkness.

However, when Bible discussions arise they identify themselves as insincere followers of Jesus. Let me give you a few examples.

Several months ago, in the Sunday school class we attend, the lesson was in Matthew 22 – The Parable of the Wedding Feast. I suggest you read the entire parable, but in essence Jesus told the story about people invited to the wedding feast, with a parallel application to those invited to redemption. The teacher began the lesson by saying, "The kingdom of heaven may be compared to a king who gave a wedding feast for his son." (Matthew 22:2) Plainly, Jesus was teaching a comparison between celebrating the wedding feast of the Groom (Jesus) and His Bride (the church). Many were invited, but few came.

The entire lesson directly related the event, the invited, and those who responded. Again, the teaching in the parable is an illustration of those invited to respond to Jesus and witness the Great Wedding Feast of the book of Revelation.

Toward the end of the parable Jesus spoke of an individual arriving improperly clothed for a wedding feast. In verses 12-14 Jesus said,

> *"'But when the king came in to look over the dinner guests, he saw a man there who was not dressed in wedding clothes, and he said to him', 'Friend, how did you come in here without wedding clothes?' And the man was speechless. 'Then the king said to the servants, 'Bind him hand and foot, and throw him into the outer darkness; in that place there will be weeping and gnashing of teeth. For many are called, but few are chosen.'"* (Matthew 22:11–15)

The verses 11-15 plainly indicate that unless one is properly dressed with the robe of righteous, one cannot enter the Kingdom of God, but are condemned to the place of "outer darkness" or hell. The response of a couple of people greatly disturbed the entire Bible study. Two individuals said Jesus was being too hard on someone.

You see, "Shadow Walkers" are those individuals perhaps slightly walking in the light of Jesus and partially walking in the darkness of Satan. Of course, I cannot say for sure, only God knows their heart, but the truth of the matter is believers are known by their words and deeds. The individuals of this response seemed to be deeply troubled with the idea of "eternal reward" and Jesus singling out individuals who do not measure up to the standard He set.

"Shadow Walkers" generally seem be people who:

- **Have an intellectual or brainy approach to the Word of God**. They may know the Word in their head, but cannot connect it to their heart (actions). They miss heaven by 12 inches, the distance between the heart and the brain. This may also be called – Theoretical Christianity.

- **Take the world's view over Scriptures.** One example is our nation's struggle with abortion. Is it murder or a woman's right to choose? Woman's choice may be a constitutional right, but it is not right in the eyes of God as revealed in Scriptures.

- **They are spectators instead of participants.** I heard a friend once say, "One can read all the books on how to be an Olympic swimmer, but without getting in the water, you're just another anchor." Another minister was heard to say about the pews, "This ain't no football game and those ain't no bleachers!" There are plenty of by-standers both inside and outside of the church. But getting personally involved in the ministry of the church as given by Christ Himself, no thanks.

- **Live one way at work and home and another with their church family.** The New Testament calls these people "hypocrites". The original Greek word "ὑποκριτής [hupokrites /hoop·ok·ree·tace/] means insincere or pretender.

In William Shakespeare's plays there were no women, only men. So, the men would have to put on "false faces" to mimic women. Their true nature was hidden or you might say they were pretenders or professional hypocrites.

These "Shadow Walkers" put on false faces. While dressing and acting, temporarily, as the righteous, they have inwardly rotten souls. Jesus dealt harshly with the "self-righteous Pharisees" and called them whitewashed tombs. *He accused them, "Woe to you, scribes and Pharisees, hypocrites! For you are like whitewashed tombs which on the outside appear beautiful, but inside they are full of dead men's bones and all uncleanness."* (Matthew 23:27)

> *"Shadow Walkers" put on false faces*

The Pharisees were a group of very powerful men charged with keeping the purity of Judaism. They paid strict attention to their customs and traditions and had an extremely rigid set of rules. Jesus accused the men of looking righteous on the outside (whitewashed tombs) while remaining unholy (unrighteous) on the inside, this full of dead men's bones and all uncleanness."

One deacon, in the church we attend, was trying to get a handle on how to convince engineers to follow Jesus. He believes with all of his heart that we have to convince people of the existence of God and prove He exists and is not a made-up figment of someone's imagination. When faith was brought into the discussion, he said, "That's not enough." Despite the Scriptures on faith, he still refused and told me, "You have too much faith."

There are so many ways to identify "Shadow Walkers", but the first criterion is by prayer. Pray about your own life and how well you live before Christ, otherwise you become a judge and will be judged as you judge other. Seek out the Lord God on how you might minister to a "Shadow Walker" and lead them toward the light of Christ. We never know all of the details, but God does. Depend upon Him.

A friend said this about ""Shadow Walkers", "Do you see the light in the distance or are you getting a sunburn?"

Let me encourage you. If you have been walking in the shadow of Jesus instead of His Light there is hope and a future for you walking in the Light. The Epistles of John (John 1,2, and 3) were a revelation by the Holy Spirit to John regarding fellowship with our church family and God.

> *"This is the message we have heard from Him and announce to you, that God is Light, and In Him there is no darkness at all. If we say that we have fellowship with Him and yet walk in the darkness, we lie and do not practice the truth; but if we walk in the Light as He Himself is in the Light, we have fellowship with one another, and the blood of Jesus His Son cleanses us from all sin. If we say that we have no sin, we are deceiving ourselves and the truth is not in us. <u>If we confess our sins</u>, He is faithful and righteous to forgive us our sins and to cleanse us from all unrighteousness. If we say that we have not sinned, we make Him a liar and His word is not in us."* (1 John 1:5–10)

The first emphasis of this passage is on "confessing our sins". Confessing simply means we agree with God. Our hearts and minds must be in agreement with God's Word. Confession, in this case is not telling your priest or pastor the sins you have committed. Confession is allowing God to show you your sins, and to feel the weight of your wrongdoing in light of God's love and mercy.

I vividly remember the evening I came to the point of deciding whether or not I would follow Jesus in redemption. When the pastor made the call to respond or invitation I already felt a very large weight of my guilt for my sin. I sat in the pew weeping as if I had lost a deeply loved parent. My fingers were glued to the pew in front of me, but the Spirit was calling, and I felt I had no option but to respond.

That evening I surrendered my life to Jesus and asked Him to save me. That night He did! I cannot adequately describe the peace that enveloped my soul, but to say the war between me and God had been settled by the "treaty of surrender" in my life. During the next ten years, as I sensed God speaking, I responded and watched Him begin the transformation of my life.

> **Jesus' died as a sacrifice for our sin.**

Confession is the result of God's Holy Spirit revealing to you how you have fallen short of God's expectations or His commandments. In chapter 2, John goes into more details about walking in darkness. He said,

> *"My little children, I am writing these things to you so that you may not sin. And if anyone sins, we have an Advocate with the Father, Jesus Christ the righteous; and He Himself is the propitiation for our sins; and not for ours only, but also for those of the whole world. By this we know that we have come to know Him, if we keep His commandments. The one who says, "I have come to know Him," and does not keep His commandments, is a liar, and the truth is not in him; but whoever keeps His word, in him the love of God has truly been perfected. By this we know that we are in Him: the one who says he abides in Him ought himself to walk in the same manner as He walked."* (1 John 2:1–6)

This passage is very clear. One cannot continue to live in sin and walk with God simultaneously. John identifies that a person does not have to sin, a willful decision, but when we sin, willfully or accidentally, we do have someone to intercede on our behalf – Jesus. He is our "advocate"

In many cultures and languages and advocate is a defense attorney that pleads the case of the guilty before a magistrate or judge. This person is Jesus! John continues by saying Jesus is the "propitiation" for our sins. Let me attempt to explain the big word "propitiation". It means a reconciler, or one who settles a debt. In regard to mankind and God, it means a sacrifice for forgiveness. We are born a sinner and unless otherwise reversed by redemption through Christ Jesus, we will die a sinner and face an eternity separated from God, never to be in His presence and confined to hell.

Technically, propitiation means the removal of wrath by the offering of a gift. The Scriptures show us a person walking in sin is at war with God. God is the offended One. We offend God with our sin and this creates a debt or something we owe God. The only way to settle a sin debt to God is by blood. In the Old Testament, a blood sacrifice was made for a person's forgiveness of sin. This was done on the Day of Atonement in which a person brought an animal to the priest for a sacrifice and burned on the altar.

In the New Testament, Jesus became our atonement. He was and is our blood sacrifice for the forgiveness of sin. Jesus' death and spilling of blood satisfies once and for all time our need to be reconciled to a Holy God by the washing away of our sin. If one walks outside the light of Christ, we are not reconciled to The One Holy God.

> ***"without the shedding of blood there is no forgiveness."*** (Hebrews 9:22)

There is so much written in the Scriptures about the idea of "shadow walking" that it is impossible to ignore it. Why then do so many continue in this lifestyle?

> *"The one who says, 'I have come to know Him,' and does not keep His commandments, is a liar, and the truth is not in him; but whoever keeps His word, in him the love of God has truly been perfected."* (1 John 2:4-5)

In the following chapters, the Truth from God's Word will be examined, encouragement will be given and perhaps lives even changed. The idea of changed lives is precisely and ultimately what the Lord God wants for each of us. He wants our lives to be one that is always adjusting to Him.

Cost of being a "Shadow Walker"

- **You walk through life on your own without the power of the Lord God**
- **You face obstacles and life itself in your own strength**
- **Decisions are made without the involvement and guidance of the Holy Spirit**
- **A person is powerless compared to the power given to God's children through redemption and commitment**
- **There's an unsettled restlessness that cannot seem to be quenched**
- **Peace is sought through materialistic methods such as boats, cars, and the accumulation of goods.**
- **You are on your own. Salvation and heaven is not in your future.**
- **People and churches walk aimlessly without purpose and success**
- **The church is just an address on Google Maps**
- **Many churches exists they have no vision, no real purpose for existing, no real fruit to show for their efforts**
- **Their budget is probably shrinking because their congregation is shrinking and there are either no plans to obediently respond to Jesus by doing evangelism and**

discipleship or they do not have the leadership of the Holy Spirit to discern how to go about doing it.

The Cost for Shadow Walking list is almost endless, but the overarching benefit of walking in the light is this:

The presence of Almighty God lives in you and you have a peace that cannot be described. Because of God's presence the cost of Shadow Walking has been replaced by God's loving provisions and presence.

Are you ready?

5 THE LIGHT COMES TO US

"And the Word became flesh, and dwelt among us, and we saw His glory, glory as of the only begotten from the Father, full of grace and truth." (John 1:14)

Throughout history, mankind has always looked up for a source of light. We have looked to the sun, the moon and the stars for God's light. Sure, we can make our own light with a fire, but this light is temporary and dependent upon someone tending the fire and adding fuel on a regular basis.

Man-made fire can warm a frozen body on a cold night and give a small amount of light but cannot be duplicated, as the bright light God created. Man can build light towers but once we leave the influence of a particular light, once again we are walking in darkness.

Let me give you an example. Have you ever driven way out of the city in the country and found darkness so thick that the headlights of your car weren't truly enough? This light source is limited in the power and field of illumination. Too many people have hit wildlife because they couldn't see the poor animals coming.

So far, we have read where the Lord God Almighty created light for the benefit of His creation, humanity. When the Creator was finished He pronounced it "good."

We moved from light and discussed darkness or the absence of light. This darkness is a representation of the absence of God's light.

Then we discussed the shadows, neither light nor darkness, but somewhere in between. Here, life can still exist, but without the power of light and leaves a person unable to operate fully.

Now we begin to discuss the Light coming to us. In this chapter we are not discussing the light from a bulb, a fire or the night sky. We are talking about the eternal, life-giving light of hope to all of mankind. The first light is temporary, lasting only a few hours each day. God's Light never ceases to illuminate our way.

In the Old Testament it is a known fact that the Hebrews (Israel) had to repeat a ceremonial observance of the Day of Atonement for the forgiveness of sin. Then the Heavenly Father provided an eternal source of that forgiveness – Jesus. His blood once and for all atoned or paid the price for our sins. Now the light God provided in the heavens, is temporary at best, it is made permanent and available at any time of the day, through Christ Jesus.

As previously mentioned God is not partially organized, but fully organized. God is not the god of confusion, but the God of order. When the time was right, He sent His only Son Jesus to give a light showing the way to God's order, and how to successfully walk in His ways.

We will be studying John's Gospel with other Scriptures to support our study. This chapter is dedicated to the Light coming to us. This is a warm and beautiful expression of God's love for you and me.

The beginning of John Gospel is called the prolog. This short passage in the first chapter reemphasizes the Creation even and the deity of Jesus.

All four Gospels begin by placing Jesus within a historical setting, but the Gospel of John is unique in the way it opens. The Book of Matthew begins with the genealogy of Jesus that connects Him to David and Abraham. Mark starts with the preaching of John the Baptist. Luke has a dedication of his work to Theophilus and follows that with a prediction of the birth of John the Baptist. But John begins with a theological prologue. It is almost as if John had said, "I want you to consider Jesus in His teaching and deeds. But you will not understand the good news of Jesus in its fullest sense unless you view Him from this point of view. Jesus is God made known or revealed in the flesh, and His words and deeds are those of the God-Man.

"The Word" is a Greek word λόγος (logos, pronounced **log·**os). In the Old Testament the Jews knew the Scriptures were the very words of God. The words or Scriptures contained the character, the purposes and the will of God as revealed to His people.

> *"In the beginning was the Word, and the Word was with God, and the Word was God. He was in the beginning with God. All things came into being through Him, and apart from Him nothing came into being that has come into being. In Him was life, and the life was the Light of men."* (John 1:1–4)

John was given by a revelation of God, the book of Revelation. He had been in the closest circle of Jesus' followers along with Peter and James. John seemed to have an especially close relationship with Jesus and God called John to pen the Gospel of John, and the Epistles of John 1, 2 and 3.

John's relationship with Jesus was such that he was shown many great truths. One of these truths were Jesus Christ is the eternal Word (verses 1–2). He existed in the beginning, not because He had a beginning as a creature, but because He is eternal. He is God and He was with God. *"Before Abraham was, I am"* (John 8:58).

Jesus Christ is the creative Word (verse 3). There is a parallel between John 1:1 and Genesis 1:1, the "new creation" and the "old creation." God created the worlds through His word: "And God said, 'Let there be …'!" "For He spoke, and it was done. He commanded it, and it stood firm" (Psalm 33:9). God created all things through Jesus Christ (Colossians 1:16), which means that Jesus is not a created being. He is eternal God.

While God created the heavens and the earth, the verb "was made" is perfect tense in the Greek, which means a "completed act." Creation is not an on-going process. It is finished. But, God never ceases His work in and around His creation that He loves so dearly, us!

> *"But He answered them, 'My Father is working until now, and I Myself am working.'"* (John 5:17).

Before Jesus ascended into the heavens, He prepared His followers to face the day when He would no longer walk physically with them. Jesus instructed the followers (verse 4) to remain in Jerusalem for

He promised them in a few days the Holy Spirit would arrive.

My sense is Jesus' followers would feel alone in the time between His ascension and the arrival of the Holy Spirit. Jesus, Immanuel, God with us, was gone and they would be alone. I can imagine what they felt and thought. Once we had God with us, walking among us and now we're left to ourselves. Jesus knew the Holy Spirit will continue the His work and He wanted to comfort those that followed Him by telling them, *"but you will receive power when the Holy Spirit has come upon you; and you shall be My witnesses both in Jerusalem, and in all Judea and Samaria, and even to the remotest part of the earth."* (Acts 1:8)

God's ongoing work is in the lives of believers through His Holy Spirit. (John 14:1-20; 26)

> *"I will ask the Father, and He will give you another Helper, that He may be with you forever; that is the Spirit of truth, whom the world cannot receive, because it does not see Him or know Him, but you know Him because He abides with you and will be in you. 'I will not leave you as orphans; I will come to you'. 'After a little while the world will no longer see Me, but you will see Me; because I live, you will live also'. 'In that day you will know that I am in My Father, and you in Me, and I in you.' 'But the Helper, the Holy Spirit, whom the Father will send in My name, He will teach you all things, and bring to your remembrance all that I said to you.'"*

Jesus Christ is the living Word (verse 14). He was neither a spirit when He ministered on earth, nor was His body a mere illusion. John and the other disciples each had a personal experience that convinced them of the reality of the body of Jesus (1 John 1:1–2). Even though John's emphasis is the deity of Christ, he makes it clear that the Son of God came in the flesh and was subject to the sinless infirmities of human nature.

> *Jesus Christ is the living Word*

In his Gospel, John points out that Jesus was weary (John 4:6) and thirsty (John 4:7). He groaned within (John 11:33) and openly wept

(John 11:35). On the cross, He thirsted (John 19:28), died (John 19:30), and bled (John 19:34). After His resurrection, He proved to Thomas and the other disciples that He still had a real body (John 20:24–29), a glorified body.

How was the "Word made flesh"? By the miracle of the Virgin Birth (Isaiah 7:14; Matthew 1:18–25; Luke 1:26–38). He took on Himself sinless human nature and identified with us in every aspect of life from birth to death. "The Word" was not a theoretical view of philosophy, but a real Person who could be seen, touched, and heard.

The revelation of God's glory is an important theme in the Gospel. Jesus revealed God's glory in His person, His works, and His words.

When I consider John 1:14, *"And the Word became flesh, and dwelt among us, and we saw His glory, glory as of the only gotten from the Father, full of grace and truth,"* I see the personalization of God's love for me and you. When the time was right the Word became flesh for all of us. God was not willing to allow His creation to go on any longer in its unredeemed state. So, He came to dwell among us and offer redemption to all who would be willing to accept it and apply it to their lives.

Jesus chose to step down off of His throne in a perfect eternal Heaven and step into a frail and temporary world as a man. Think about it for a minute. Who among us would want to leave family and friends that love us very much and a position with great authority with a life of extraordinary comfort to move to a remote jungle where there's no electricity, fresh water, and natives seeking to destroy us?

Jesus stepped down from a place where everything responded to His spoken Word, including all of creation. He stepped down into a world with strife, war, bigotry, hate, murder, illness and death. Sound like where I want to be! Huh?

That is precisely what Jesus did. He disrobed His Godliness to come as a mortal man with hunger, thirst, normal human desires and temptations. He became as fragile flesh and bone. He could suffer physically and even die.

You may ask why I spend so much time on this truth, but in the late First Century there appeared people called "Gnostics". These people believed they had been given a more complete and deeper truth than the mere Christian family had. The Gnostics were "all-knowing".

The Gnostics believed flesh was evil. The fact that mere skin was evil meant if Jesus was human, he was evil and could not be divine. He only appeared human. This belief rendered the fact that God became flesh and dwelt among us. This would also mean Jesus could not be God!

One might be tempted to say, "Well, this was in the First Century." Actually, it still exists today in two main-lines, world-wide "religions" of our day. Both of these religions are extremely powerful in their draw to people, but more dangerous than all of the life-threatening illnesses of the world combined because they threaten the eternity of millions.

The word "flesh" means humanity in this verse does not mean sinfulness or evilness, prone to human weaknesses, like temptations, emotions, pains of body and hunger and death itself. Think what the death of Jesus would mean if He couldn't die. The cross and the grave would have no meaning or bearing on His life. If Jesus couldn't die then He wouldn't be able to affect the blood sacrifice for you and me. There would be no death to conquer and neither would there be hope for us overcoming death into the eternal Kingdom of God. Life would crudely and cruelly end.

Jesus would have to come in the flesh to affect us. He led the way and was our model and example. He came to show us the way to live successfully, with power and victory the way God intended for humanity to live. He showed us how we might live devoted lives for our Heavenly Father. He also showed us eternity future.

Recently we re-watched the old movie, "Soylent Green". The population had exponentially grown and they people had no real source of food. The people lived in a mere existence without meaning or hope. Only a few had jobs, but many had no place to sleep. Food was rationed by the government in the form of small wafers. Water was dealt out by small amounts. The main character disturbingly discovered how the government made soylent green – "out of people". When people died their bodies were processed into food and distributed to hungry people. I cannot image living like that, without hope, without a future just mere existence. That mere existence would be the norm if Jesus did not come in the flesh, experience a death, burial and resurrection.

I thank the Heavenly Father He raised Jesus from the grave and He conquered death to be able to lead me to life eternal. Aren't you?

In Jesus' day, the Jews thought God lived in the temple. If they were away from Jerusalem, they were away from God. Isn't it slightly possible that many of us think God is only in "the church"? Thus, if we've been out of church we are absent from God. I have to be careful here because God is in the life of every believer if every believer allows Him to live within them through redemption in Christ. The church, not the building, is a group of people, our faith family, which loves us and encourages us to remain strong in Christ and to grow us, spiritually. We need them!

> *God became flesh and came to live among us*

The main point in verse 14 is "and dwelt among us". God came to move into our lives, not by force, but by invitation. The important truth is God is with us, always! Yet don't we hear prayers, "God be with them." If one is among the redeemed of Christ, God is with them! The phrase, "be with them" is a redundant, superficial, unnecessary phrase.

God came and pitched His tent with us. There are several analogies that personalize this for me. First, God became our house guest. I have had a few roommates in my college days. Some were real water buffalos. You want to talk about slobs? Additionally, they were inconsiderate of the privacy, property and needs of other roommates. I think of God as that roommate who is not invasive but cooperative.

God is the person thinking about what you need before you think of it yourself. He doesn't come and borrow sugar, He speaks it into being. There's no need to evacuate when a hurricane approaches, He calms the storm. When the lights go out (oops, forgot to pay the bill) He could do what He did at creation, He merely speaks, "Let there be light!" There's no need to call the ambulance, God is the Healer. When you are upset, He is the Comforter.

Second, God moved in next door. We have neighbors that look out for each other. Anytime they see a stranger at a neighboring home they will ask, "Can I help you?" What the neighbor is saying, "You don't belong there, what are you doing?" What better neighbor could you have than God, Himself?

Third, God set up his camping tent right next door to ours. My wife and I have tent camped for several decades. Every campsite we have met and camped beside many really good people. Campers generally look out for each other. We had neighboring campers put some of our equipment up while we were gone and a large wind storm came up.

Campers share resources and help each other. One Thanksgiving we were camping in the mountains near El Paso, Texas. There were two or three families camping nearby. One of the men came over and invited Karen and I to have Thanksgiving with them. We had a memorable and great time.

> *God dwells among us means we have a loving, watchful and providing person that has all the power and authority to accomplish anything and everything*

God dwells among us means we have a loving, watchful and providing person that has all the power and authority to accomplish anything and everything. I truthfully cannot say I have always understood this truth, but as I have walked with Him, I have found this to be a great truth in my life.

Where ever you are and whatever you are doing, God's there with you. Once, another man and I went to visit one of our church family men. When we arrived at his home he was working in the garage. As we approached the garage we noticed he was drinking a beer.

Instinctively he hid the can behind him. I simply said, "Go ahead with your beer. If you can drink in front of God you can drink in front of me. I won't condemn you." Amazingly people stop doing what they think they shouldn't be doing when they see their pastor.

Summarizing, God created light. Before God spoke light into existence, light did not exist. One day, the Light became flesh and blood because He wanted to be with us and near us all of the time and we will never grow weary of His companionship. When God became light in the flesh and blood He became available to take up residency in our lives and to dwell in us, around us and with us.

God's Light represents several key ideas. First, God's light reveals the best path for my life to take. Let me share the testimony of others:

> *"You will make known to me the path of life; In Your presence is fullness of joy; In Your right hand there are pleasures forever."* (Psalm 16:11)
>
> *"He restores my soul; He guides me in the paths of righteousness for His name's sake."* (Psalm 23:3)
>
> *"Your word is a lamp to my feet and a light to my path."* (Psalm 119:105)

There have been many times in my life that I have both asked God, "What should I do" and there have been many times, I haven't. The times I have not sought God's path for my life are those times in which I have not done as well or experienced troubles and no peace.

Sometimes we all have an attitude of I will do what I can and those things I can't do, I will pray. Many people throughout time have discovered the real benefit of seeking God's mind first instead of trusting their own opinion or wisdom. God will often give us directions that appear to not make sense, but if we trust Him and follow that plan we will see victory.

Those times I have sought the mind of God for my life's direction have been times of great reward. Some things were not highly crucial, and others were deep needs, either physical, emotional or financial.

The arrival of the Light has had many effects upon people of that day and today, including myself

> *Light gives us joy, blessings and meaning to life in the midst of adversity, sorrow and death*

The effects of the Light upon the lives of those of whom it rest upon is as individualized as the relationship with the Lord God. Jesus said, "I have come to give you abundant life. (John 10:10)

The Light has given all it has truly touched a hope for a new day and a better tomorrow. Life has a way of swerving out of control. Families have problems, marriages breakup, finances go sour and if that's not enough we may have physical health problems. Without the presence of the Light, where would we find hope for a better day? Life would continue on with a sense that we are alone, and no one cares. Life would be merely an existence, without meaning and end with a lifetime misery and despair. Yet, we who have Christ as Lord and Savior have Almighty God looking after us, loving us, caring for us and comforting us when we feel lousy or down.

When a genuine believer testifies about the blessing Jesus has given chief among them is joy which is unexplainable. Our first battle, that against God is over. Nothing on earth seems to bother anyone who belongs to the Living Lord because this is just a temporary life and we know that the Father and Son lives within us, so we never walk alone.

Another benefit of walking in the Light is having fellowship or companionship with other people who have the same Spirit of God residing within them. There is a shared compassion and love for each other that those either walking in darkness or the shadows do not possess. We pray for each other, when there's a need many respond to help their fellow believer. When one is down or depressed we can ask for prayer and wait to see God answering that need with someone's visit or phone call that lifts our spirits.

The Light gives one the blessings of facing adversity and troubles. Somehow the power and peace of Jesus gives the one in the Light the strength and endurance to face whatever adversity or sorrow they face and even death. He gives blessings instead of loneliness. Have you ever noticed God speaking to your spirit when you are down, suffering or feel alone?

As a personal testimony: I was admitted to the Heart Vascular Institute of Memorial Herman Hospital, Texas Medical Center on April 23, 2015 for heart transplant. The next seventy days were a nightmare. I was quite comfortable in the room, but I just wasn't at home and couldn't live a normal life.

I rarely thought about what I was facing. My birth heart's output had fallen to less than ten percent. It was crucial I receive a heart. There were days I felt in a funk, but God spoke to me through His Word, that I read and Christian brothers and sisters working in the unit to give me peace.

After the first offer of a heart failed, the lead cardiologist asked, "Are you ok with this?" I remember feeling absolutely at peace. I told him that no matter what, I was in a win, win, win situation. I won if God healed me, I won if I received a transplant and I won if He brought me home to be with Him.

On July 6, 2015 the Lord God gave me the heart of a nineteen-year young man. At this point my life was on borrowed time and my Heavenly Father gave me His grace one more time. God had saved my life from eight heart attacks, two by-pass surgeries and now a transplant.

There are people around the world committed to Jesus, the Light. They are in situations that many times they have a choice to publicly reject their faith in Jesus or die. Many times our brothers and sisters bravely face their own death rather than reject Jesus.

I am deeply thankful and encouraged by the fact that "the Word became flesh, and dwelt among us, and we saw His glory, glory as of the only begotten from the Father, full of grace and truth." (John 1:14)

When the Father and Son come to make their home in your, you will be empowered to do many things you were not able to do without them. After all, they are the one that created and saved you.

Don't you owe them every ounce of your life?

6 WALK IN THE LIGHT OF GOD

"Then Jesus again spoke to them, saying, 'I am the Light of the world; he who follows Me will not walk in the darkness, but will have the Light of life.'" (John 8:12)

In the previous chapters you have seen where God created the light of the heavens and their usefulness. You have seen what darkness means and I've introduced a new topic, ""Shadow Walkers" or those who walk in both the light of God and the darkness of evil. In chapter 5 you saw where the Light became flesh and dwells among us. Now we will see what it means to truly walk in the Light of Almighty God and His Son Jesus.

Within the Holy Scriptures we see where God revealed Himself, His presence and His power in light.

> Genesis 1 – creation of light
>
> Exodus 13:21 – God appeared as pillar of fire by night to guide Israel through night
>
> Matthew 17:2 – at Jesus' transfiguration his face and garments became as bright light
>
> Matthew 5:13-14 – Jesus said, "You are the salt and light"
>
> Acts 9 – At Saul's conversion Jesus showed Himself as a bright light blinding Saul
>
> Acts 13 – Peter was arrested, and an Angel of the Lord appeared in bright light and freed Him
>
> Matthew 24 – Jesus foretold that when the great tribulation comes there will be an absence of light

Light represents the presence of the Lord Jesus Christ in our lives. When Moses encounter Yhwh for the first time Jehovah God appeared in a burning bush.

In John's Gospel, we are given great truths about walking in the light that provides a person with the peace of God to walk through the darkness of this world. (Take a look at John 1:1-4, 14)

The word "Light" is from the Greek – photos (fotos) which is where we get the word photography. Photography is the collection of light on to a source. In the original Greek and to the hearers of Jesus' words it meant "the truth". Today we see many people with various degrees of "truths" but Jesus remains the One Eternal Truth sent from God. Light is a Person from God - Jesus.

The context of the setting in John 8:35 we need to remember Jesus used parables (true stories) to teach his audience the truths of God. Some of these parables began with the "I Am" statements.

> John 6:35 - When asked about bread – Jesus said, "I Am the bread of life"
>
> John 10:7 - Jesus said, "I am the door"
>
> John 10:11 - Jesus said, "I am the good shepherd"
>
> John 11:25 - Jesus said, "I am the resurrection"
>
> John 15:1 - "Jesus said, 'I am the vine'"

The great "I Am" statements are central to the identity, function, power and authority of Jesus. When Moses was charged by God to bring Israel out of bondage in Egypt, Moses said to Jehovah God,

> *"Then Moses said to God, 'Behold, I am going to the sons of Israel, and I will say to them, The God of your fathers has sent me to you. Now they may say to me, 'What is His name?' What shall I say to them?' God said to Moses, "I AM WHO I AM'; and He said, Thus you shall say to the sons of Israel, 'I AM has sent me to you.'"* (Exodus 3:13–14)

Notice here God gave Moses His name, "I Am". "I Am has sent you."

Jesus was preaching in the synagogue. The Jewish historian

Josephus tells us this was the outside of the forecourt of the temple, part of the court of the women. In this location stood two colossal golden lamp-stands, on which hung a multitude of lamps, which were lighted after the evening sacrifice (probably every evening during the feast of tabernacles) diffusing their brilliancy throughout the city. All the people of Jerusalem could see the light shining outside the synagogue.

Light to Israel indicated the presence of God. Remember Exodus 3:2 when Moses first encountered Jehovah in the burning bush that was not consumed by the first and Exodus 13:21 when Jehovah guided Israel through the desert at night by a pillar of fire.

The light is considered a "revelation" of God or an unveiling of what was previously hidden. The "I Am" statements identified Jesus' deity and said to the people, "The God (Jehovah) of your salvation and deliverance is here. "This was comforting to some people because for 7 centuries since the prophecy of Isaiah, Israel expected the Lord (Messiah) to come and deliver the nation. Some thought Jesus, the Messiah (also known as "Yeshua" - Hebrew) would come and free them as a great military leader from the occupation of the pagan Romans. At this time, the Messiah was to re-establish Israel's great power, strength and wealth, but Elijah, the prophet would have to return before the arrival of the Messiah. The long-expected return of Elijah was to usher in Israel's return to power.

> **Light is a revelation of God**

> *"Behold, I am going to send you Elijah the prophet before the coming of the great and terrible day of the LORD. 'He will restore the hearts of the fathers to their children and the hearts of the children to their fathers, so that I will not come and smite the land with a curse.'"* (Malachi 4:5–6)

The "I Am" statements set the stage for a lot of speculation and false expectations.

> *"And His disciples asked Him, 'Why then do the scribes say that Elijah must come first?' And He answered and said,*

> *'Elijah is coming and will restore all things; but I say to you that Elijah already came, and they did not recognize him, but did to him whatever they wished. So, also the Son of Man is going to suffer at their hands.' Then the disciples understood"* (Matthew 17: 10-13)

However, in the context of the Scriptures, Jesus said, *"I am the Light of the world; he who follows Me will not walk in the darkness but will have the Light of life."* (John 8:12) In verses 3-11 the scribes and Pharisees brought a woman caught in adultery. Verse 6 identifies the religious leaders' motives, *"to test him so they might have grounds for accusing Him"*. They hoped to discredit him either way, for the Law of Moses demanded she be put to death by stoning. If Jesus said, "stone her" He would be stepping of His character and if he dismissed her punishment He would be guilty of relaxing moral standard. After they continued to badger Jesus, He said, *"He who is without sin among you, let him be the first to throw a stone at her."* (John 8:7) Then Jesus told her to repent by saying, *"Go and sin no more."* (verse 11)

This setting brought up the great revelation in John 8:12, *"I am the Light of the world; he who follows Me will not walk in the darkness but will have the Light of life."* Those present knew exactly what Jesus was referring to. The lady had been caught in adultery. She was considered evil or walking in darkness. Yet Jesus was there as the Light of God showing the way to righteousness and walking in the companionship of Almighty God.

Jesus' revelation to His divine identity would be cause for Israel's religious leaders to begin to think of Jesus as a threat. The scribes and Pharisees would continue their harassment of Jesus until they got what they wanted, Jesus silenced by death, which was the punishment for blasphemy or slandering God.

The Light of God's Word and presence shines the truth on evil. This is like saying, give a man rope and he will hang himself. People may hide their true character for a while, but it is impossible to keep the camouflage up for ever. These religious leaders showed their true character and Jesus told them, *"You are from below, I am from above; you are of this world, I am not of this world. "Therefore, I said to you that you will die in your sins; for unless you believe that I am He, you will die in your sins."* (John 8:23–24)

Jesus, here, was identifying the religious leaders of that day as evil and walking in darkness. Darkness which is a symbol of evil, sin, and ignorance (Isaiah 9:2; Matthew 4:16; 27:45; and John 3:19). "Light" in the Bible is a symbol of God and His holiness (Acts 9:3; 1 John 1:5). Jesus is "the Light," not merely a light or another light among many lights. He is the only Light, "the true Light" (John 1:9), for the whole world.[1]

Jesus made a concrete stand about living in sin verses righteousness. Basically, this is an issue of choice and lifestyle. People choose whether they will walk in darkness or light. Despite the popular modern belief that, "Jesus understands my life" and dismisses sin is a lie. Like the woman caught in adultery He will call unrighteous living sin.

I want you to image for a moment. Your life is over and you are standing before the judgment seat of Christ and He asked you, "Why should I let you into Heaven?" What would you say? Suppose another scenario. Jesus asked you to justify your lifestyle. How do you think you'd respond? Would you say it was because of my upbringing? It was because of my job? Or a favorite of Adam in the Garden of Eden, "It's that woman's fault that You gave me. She's the problem."

Society seems to be following the pattern of the more technological we become the better we are at making excuses. When the woman was caught in adultery she made no excuses. I believe she somehow recognized "the Light" had shined upon her life and the jig was up. She had been exposed and there was no excuse.

Light represents the Lord God shining the truth upon His character, His ways, His purposes and His plans. Do you truly believe God knows at the next intersection which way you will turn, given a choice? I do.

Do you believe that God orchestrates each turn, every decision and direction of our lives? I don't! I do not accept that Almighty God violates His character of giving us a free choice. Let me explain. He knows what decisions you will make based upon His eternal nature and being outside of time itself, but what He wants more than anything is that you and I ask Him for direction and follow the instructions He gives us.

If God forces us to follow His will then isn't He a puppeteer? Aren't we at the end of strings? When God gives a command, we have a choice – obey or disobey. There is no middle ground. One writer once said, "Delayed obedience is disobedience." So, when God gives us instructions the time to respond is immediately, not tomorrow (mañana). The situation of tomorrow never comes.

Responding to the Light does take a great deal of resolve. One must say to one's self, "I am going to do what I sense God telling me to do, no matter what." As you hear the small voice speaking in your spirit, you may be tempted to ask, "Is this God?" My first suggest would be accept it, but make sure what you're hearing fits in with the character, person, and revealed will of The Lord through His Word. Secondly, do what He's told you to do. We truly come to know God as we obey Him. So, the next time you hear from the Heavenly Father you will sense His voice quicker and know Him more thoroughly and find blessings.

Personally, I see faith as ultimately an action. A lot of people say, "No it's not!" But in Hebrews 11 we see accounts of how people heard from God, acted upon what they heard and accomplished the plans and purposes of the Lord God. I like Noah. He could have said, "Build a what? Put what in it?" Instead God gave Noah explicit engineering details and as a result Noah's belief in the One who spoke to him saved his own family and two of all the animals on earth.

Faith must be the primary action of a follower of Jesus. It is by faith we're saved.

> *"For by grace you have been saved through faith; and that not of yourselves, it is the gift of God; not as a result of works, so that no one may boast."* (Ephesians 2:8–9)

If you were to examine all of the miracles of Jesus in the Gospels you would find faith as the driving power behind the healings.

> Mathew 9:2   Some men brought a paralyzed friend to Jesus
>
> Matthew 9:20-22   A woman who had hemorrhaged for 12 years
>
> Matthew 9:27-29   Two blind men

There were so many who had their lives changed "because of their faith". They believed with every ounce of their being that Jesus was the answer to their sufferings. My own experience was over 27 years. I had 8 heart attacks, two by-pass surgeries and a pacemaker. The doctors said it was a genetic defect. But the Merciful God sent me to a cardiologist who immediately saw the need and I was approved for a heart transplant. By the time of the transplant, my cardiac function was less than ten percent. On July 6, 2015, My Hope gave me a 19 year old heart which functions as a healthy 19 year old heart. The Light responded in my life because I had given it to Him and lived for Him, sins warts and all.

> *Peoples' lives are changed by their faith in Jesus*

7 HOW CAN I WALK IN THE LIGHT OF GOD?

"He who has My commandments and keeps them is the one who loves Me; and he who loves Me will be loved by My Father, and I will love him and will disclose Myself to him." (John 14:21)

There are a lot of reasons why people "go to church". For some it is a social gathering where they meet people their same age many of which are facing the same issues in life. They are able to find out how each other are doing, share their ailments and have great fellowships (eatin' meetin'). We need socialization and we need people to care for us and allow us to care for them and pray for us.

Another reason why some "go to church" is they've done their thing for God. I have actually been told this several times. This reason seems to contain the idea that God needs something from us. There is something we can do to improve God's life or fulfill it. One day after hearing this I responded by saying, "There's nothing I can do for God. He existed just fine before I was born and will do well after I die." God spoke everything into existence long before He created the first human being. If anything, God wants us, so He can love us.

There is a group who "go to church" in hopes of pleasing a Holy God. They may do great works, serve on committees or even pastor a church, but pleasing God? The Scriptures give us the truth about pleasing God, *"without faith it is impossible to please Him, for he who comes to God must believe that He is and that He is a rewarder of those who seek Him."* (Hebrews 11:6) If you want to see The Light you must have a concrete belief in His existence and a willingness to come into agreement, both body and mind, with the Word of God.

The Logos (Word) of God is His revelation of Himself to us. The Word is the lifeblood to a follower of Jesus. It becomes something that's not merely on our minds occasionally, but on our hearts constantly. This is the definition of meditating on the Word. The Psalmist wrote:

> *"How blessed is the man who does not walk in the counsel of the wicked, Nor stand in the path of sinners, Nor sit in the seat of scoffers! But his delight is in the law of the LORD, And in His law he meditates day and night. He will be like a tree firmly planted by streams of water, Which yields its fruit in its season And its leaf does not wither; And in whatever he does, he prospers. The wicked are not so, But they are like chaff which the wind drives away. Therefore, the wicked will not stand in the judgment, Nor sinners in the assembly of the righteous. For the LORD knows the way of the righteous, But the way of the wicked will perish."* (Psalm 1:1–6)

> **The Word of God is His revelation of Himself to us**

Far East mysticism religions speak of meditation. I sometimes wonder if followers of Jesus see meditation in light of the Far Eastern religions. My unsophisticated way of defining "meditation" is to think upon, reflect, to ponder, to pray about, to ask God questions about its meaning and application. This occurs more in the Old Testament, but I am one that sees no difference in God's truth from the Old Testament through the New Testament. To meditate upon the Word of God is to focus on Him.

> *When we spend quality time in God's Word, we begin to know God more intimately.*

One prevailing thought is reading the Bible. We may read it at some break-neck speed. We can find ourselves reading from Genesis 1:1 to Revelation 22 and at this speed. At that speed we will discern "some" spiritual insights. We also teach in many of our churches to spend some quality time with the Lord, but we all know that our Heavenly Father wants to spend some quality time with us.

Let me give you an example. In our quick-paced world we have texting now. Someone may send you a sentence or two, but as far as having a meaningful conversation with them, who has the time. More and more people want to spend quality time with their friends, relatives and especially their family. They don't want a sentence that says, "doing fine, how are you?"

For those have grown children, a casual stop by your house is fine occasionally, but you would prefer to spend an afternoon or evening. It is great to have more than one generation stuffing their faces together and afterwards talking about life.

Our life with God is no different. He doesn't want us to stop by on the way to the store. He wants to sit down and talk a while. Reading the Bible is a fine exercise, but meditating on the message contained within is more important. When we spend time deep in the Word of God and allow Him to speak to our hearts we begin to see His nature, His pleasure and how our lives are fitting in with His revealed will.

The idea of meditating upon the Word of God is not spoken of, as such, in the New Testament. You can be sure that Jesus spent quality time in prayer when He was alone. He probably thought deeply about what the Word of God said to Him.

Walking in the Light of Jesus is not something one can do like at eating at a fast-food restaurant

The Apostle Paul wrote to the Philippian church an reprimand to think deeper about the truth of God. He wrote:

> "Finally, brethren, whatever is true, whatever is honorable, whatever is right, whatever is pure, whatever is lovely, whatever is of good repute, if there is any excellence and if anything, worthy of praise, dwell on these things." (Philippians 4:8)

The word "dwell" indicates that we are to be spend considerable time reflecting upon that which is worthy. (λογίζομαι –logizomai, pronounced log·**id**·zom·ahee) means to consider, weigh, meditate on. As Christians we face a world so negative and hostile to the Gospel that we need more time to "take God's Word in account, to weight out what the Scriptures tells us or to spend time focusing on what it is saying to us.

My wife tells me I have too much time to think. Let me translate or clarify. When the Holy Spirit puts an idea on my mind I may spend months praying about it. My desire is to get to know the Lord God more intimately; to see how my life measures up to His Will and evaluate what I need to do in response. I have found meditation to be a great source of comfort, my personal discipleship and insight into God's truths.

Walking in the Light of Jesus isn't something one can do at the drive-through at a fast-food restaurant. The Holy Spirit may whet your appetite in Bible study or worship but I have found it highly beneficial to go home, get a few resources out and study it in more depth. When I do this, I am actually double checking the person that presented the study or sermon. You might say, "I'd never do that. It is disrespectful!"

> **Walking in the light takes time and determination**

Every believer needs to examine, on their own, what they have been taught at a church meeting. Our eternity or daily life is at stake. The Apostle Paul was encouraging the Berean Church with an example of this very truth:

> *"The brethren immediately sent Paul and Silas away by night to Berea, and when they arrived, they went into the synagogue of the Jews. Now these were more noble-minded than those in Thessalonica, for they received the word with great eagerness, examining the Scriptures daily to see whether these things were so."* (Acts 17:10-11)

Paul and Silas, as usual, went to the synagogue and sought out the Jews and presented them with the Gospel truth. Dr. Luke details the Berean church "was more noble-minded and received the world with great eagerness." While biblical presentation should be exciting to a believer, it should also be sound doctrine and it is the believers' duty to "examine the Scriptures to see whether these things are so."

This is where a deeper study of Scriptures benefits the believer. When a near truth or not-so-near truth is presented it should sound an alarm within us.

Recently I heard a pastor describe a meeting he attended, and he said, "the person was a Jesus seeker." Instantly a red flag went up. I turned to my wife and said, "The Scriptures say no man seeks after God." To quote what I showed her, *"There is none who understands, There is none who seeks for God;"* (Romans 3:11)

Now let me share something: when the Holy Spirit begins to move in one's life, the person will seek to understand God. I have found this truth many times in people recently redeemed and freshly filled with the Holy Spirit. They have a hunger and thirst for God's righteousness and how to live with victory and power in the Kingdom of God.

I have gone into great detail for one purpose only, to show the reader that following the Light is not a casual lifestyle. A follower of Jesus is busy praying, studying the Scriptures, fellowshipping with other more mature believers, worship and ministry. You have been presented with many things to ponder and pray about. However, it isn't to fill pages of a book, but to answer the question in the title of this chapter. **How Can I walk in the Light of Almighty God and His Son Jesus?**

For the remaining discussion of this chapter we will move to John's Gospel, chapter 14.

John 14:16–24. Much of the discussion will center around verse 21 and verse 23.

Jesus was preparing the disciples for His soon-coming departure. Typically people do not like change. They may say they need change but an opinion poll usually reveals change is alright for someone else, but I want to remain the same.

Whether the pastor senses a change in direction to reach and disciple the lost, and the church has been in decline for years and the body of Christ knows something must change, they will say this, "Well you shouldn't change the Gospel." What they are actually saying, "We don't want to change to be obedient to Jesus."

In church renewal work I have encountered this many times. But the most difficult truth to communicate is that no one wants to change the message, only how we carry on the mission of the church. The church should be centered around five functions: worship, ministry, evangelism, discipleship and fellowship, and in that order.

There has been too much research by denominations that indicate changes that need to take place in the 21st Century church and it seems to fall mainly on deaf eyes or hard hearts. Change is inevitable. We age, isn't that change? Our taste in music and movies varies, isn't that change? Our priorities in life even changes. Life is a cycle of change.

So why are we talking about change in the subject of following the Light? Because so many instances of individuals and churches must change to walk in the Light of Jesus. Verses 16 – 24 probably indicate a great change on the horizon for many churches and individuals.

I will not go into extreme details about the changes that need to take place in the life of the believer and the church, but to say this truth: one cannot do what they've done for years that didn't work and expect different results.

> *There are many false beliefs in the lives of people in the church*

One lady in a church I was leading in revitalization told me, "Heck, God's just going to drop people in these chairs!" Please don't think I left that lie from Satan go unchallenged. My response was, "So why are so few people in this church? Why hasn't God "just dropped people in the chairs?" That is not the plan I see in Scriptures. We are given a commandment to go and make disciples. (Matthew 28:18-20) Have you as a church done this?"

There are many pastors, at least within my home church denomination that appears to be courageous and bold in the power of the Lord and lead their churches to function in the power and victory of Christ. These men will watch their churches slowly die and the people will ask, "What happened?"

Year after year, city after city is experiencing a growing number of churches that simply dwindle down to no one. Each year the pastor buries another strong, mature believer. The leadership is dying off and no one is replacing them. CAUTION: This is not the case in all churches. There are many churches outgrowing their facilities. What's the difference? The failing churches have lost their vision as to why they exist and the growing churches have been reinvigorated by a fresh vision from the Lord. The growing churches focus on the Lord and connecting people with Him. The dying church is on life support and waiting for the last heartbeat. There is a tendency to be complacent on "inside" benefits and activities rather than focusing on the outward, soul-reaching, life-changing ministry of outreach.

Let me put it on a more individual focus. People, if not challenged will over time grow spiritually stale. The Apostle Paul told young pastor Timothy

> *"I solemnly charge you in the presence of God and of Christ Jesus, who is to judge the living and the dead, and by His appearing and His kingdom: preach the word; be ready in season and out of season; reprove, rebuke, exhort, with great patience and instruction. For the time will come when they will not endure sound doctrine; but wanting to have their ears tickled, they will accumulate for themselves teachers in accordance to their own desires, and will turn away their ears from the truth and will turn aside to myths. But you, be sober in all things, endure hardship, do the work of an evangelist, fulfill your ministry."* (2 Timothy 4:1–5)

Almost all that I have shared with you, I have heard many times. But these verses still apply. God's Word is timeless. The Word of God always has application to our lives today.

We appear to be living in these times of verse 3-4 right now. There are so many within churches that wants to hear "sweet lullabies" of sermons rather than being spiritually challenged. They want to be told how well their lives are and how successful their church is and God is pleased. I, personally, am not into back pats, either giving or receiving. True pastors have off days when they're preaching. But to live in that mode, something is wrong.

Eventually, people will get use to the sermon lullabies and can sit comfortably in the pew. I had an older evangelist tell me one day, "If you ever hear someone say, 'You stepped on my toes today.' Remind them their toes were in the wrong place." Being politically correct does not go with the Gospel message. In John, chapter 21, Jesus asked Peter three questions,

> *If you love Jesus you will search the Scriptures to learn His will and commands*

> *"So, when they had finished breakfast, Jesus said to Simon Peter, 'Simon, son of John, do you love Me more than these?' He said to Him, 'Yes, Lord; You know that I love You.' He said to him, 'Tend My lambs.' He said to him again a second time, 'Simon, son of John, do you love Me?' He said to Him, 'Yes, Lord; You know that I love You.' He said to him, 'Shepherd My sheep.' He said to him the third time, 'Simon, son of John, do you love Me?' Peter was grieved because He said to him the third time, 'Do you love Me?' And he said to Him, 'Lord, you know all things; You know that I love You.' Jesus said to him, 'Tend My sheep.'"* (John 21:15-17)

All three questions were not the same. The first question was, "Do you love me more than these?"

Clearly Jesus was talking about the other disciples. Setting the scene: Jesus had already risen from the grave. A few days later the disciples decided to go fishing. Jesus appeared on shore and when the disciple arrived Jesus had a fire going with fish. (21:9). Then Jesus invited the disciples to come and have breakfast. (21:12)

When the breakfast meal was finished Jesus asked Peter, "Simon, son of John, do you love Me more than these? (21:15) This question was in response to Peter's bold statement just prior to Jesus' arrest, trial and crucifixion, as seen in Matthew 26:33-35)

> *"But Peter said to Him, 'Even though all may fall away because of You, I will never fall away.' Jesus said to him, 'Truly I say to you that this very night, before a rooster crows, you will deny Me three times.' Peter said to Him, 'Even if I have to die with You, I will not deny You.' All the disciples said the same thing too.'"*

Peter had earlier denied knowing Jesus. Now, Jesus was restoring Peter, by allowing him to make a public statement. Peter had been given a choice, whether he could love Jesus more than the other disciples. This is an important question for all believers. But Jesus was giving Peter the opportunity to place his relationship with Jesus ahead of anyone else. This would later prove to be important because Peter had to choose between his loyalty to Jesus and the officials that had ordered Peter to stop preaching Jesus, which landed him in jail.

"Peter answered, 'Yes, Lord; You know that I love You.' He said to him, 'Tend My lambs.' This verb, "tend" actually comes from the Greek meaning, "cause them to eat." The three questions with Peter's three responses indicate Jesus called Peter to "feed the sheep" the Word of God and "to shepherd" or lead them in paths of righteousness.

So, you see, Paul's warning and encouragement to Pastor Timothy was a sound and divine instruction to Timothy (2 Timothy 4:1–5) and every pastor today. Those who proclaim the Good News are called to give their flock a healthy diet of God's Word (feed) and guide them in their spiritual development, not give them pastoral favorites that fail to challenge the congregation. Did you ever feed your children what was good for them or did you allow them to eat junk? If you love your children you feed them what they need, not what they want. The same truth applies to a New Testament church.

Paul's letter to the Galatian church might be comforting to some and disturbing to others, but your pastor is not your pastor by your choice. He belongs to God and was sent from God to feed and shepherd the flock.

> *Paul, an apostle not sent from men nor through the agency of man, but through Jesus Christ and God the Father, who raised Him from the dead,"* (Galatians 1:1)

The sermon should be spiritually challenging, and the people will become accustomed to lifting of the name of Jesus. In fact, there is a lot of research showing Millennials avoid the "organized church" because it so little resembles the message of the Bible and the ministry of Christ. They want the genuine deal. Millennials aren't afraid of the truth of God, but they are tired of the emphasis of money in the offering to support huge building and salary expenditures that have nothing to do with reaching people. My pastor would take exception with this statement because he seems to be operating in the post-World War 2 era (or error) that if you build a church, the people will come."

> **Sermons should challenge you rather than entertain you. God desires we respond to His Word!**

What happens in the absence of light? One might say people gravitate toward the "Shadow Walking" or "darkness". I know you're saying people don't lose their salvation. You caught me! The genuinely redeemed do not lose their salvation but thrive in the presence of Jesus and grow spiritually; sometimes despite the work of the church they attend.

A couple of years ago, I called a friend who is a minister and former missionary to Brazil. We have worked together on a church revitalization team for several years. I needed wise counsel and I asked him, "Is it possible the reason why pastors are not leading their church in obedience to the Lord because they themselves are not walking in the light?" I will give you the answer later.

> **Light gives joy, blessings and meaning to life in the midst of adversity, sorrow and death**

Whatever the reason, we're witnessing a record number of church closures in the United States. "An estimated 800-900 in our denomination face closure each year.

Nationwide that number rises to well over 3,000." (According to Bob Bickford in a September 17, 2015 report, Bob is a Replant pastor, the associate director of Replant for the North American Mission Board, and serves as the chair of the Church Revitalization Team of the St. Louis Metro Baptist Association.) Isn't that alarming?

There is one God, one Spirit, one Lord (1 Corinthians 12:4-6) and one Light, Jesus. I will detail the role of the Light shortly, but Jesus, the Light shines on the truth of God's Word and the health of His church. So how can some churches be thriving while others are dying? One thought I heard many years ago before the church death cancer began to spread so aggressively is this, "If the Holy Spirit removes Himself from the presence of the church, most could continue to operate in their own strength for ten to twenty years before the headstone is place over it."

Now concerning the question I asked a couple of paragraphs ago. My missionary – pastor friend said, He believed this is precisely the problem. The leaders of the church are not abiding or living in the light, so they are unable to see the truth that Jesus shines on their own lives or the lives of their churches. I am not the sharpest tool in the shed, but there is help for these churches which the pastors will not call upon. A local pastor told me, "My church doesn't need revitalization." My question to him was, "Is your church thriving in bringing lives to redemption and discipling them? Is your church experiencing the moving of God within the congregation? He honestly answered, "No."

Now that I have primed the pump, let's discuss the focus of John 14:16-24 (Verses 21; 23)

> *'I will ask the Father, and He will give you another Helper, that He may be with you forever; that is the Spirit of truth, whom the world cannot receive, because it does not see Him or know Him, but you know Him because He abides with you and will be in you. 'I will not leave you as orphans; I will come to you. 'After a little while the world will no longer see Me, but you will see Me; because I live, you will live also. 'In*

that day you will know that I am in My Father, and you in Me, and I in you. ***'He who has My commandments and keeps them is the one who loves Me; and he who loves Me will be loved by My Father, and I will love him and will disclose Myself to him.'*** *Judas (not Iscariot) said to Him, 'Lord, what then has happened that You are going to disclose Yourself to us and not to the world?'* ***Jesus answered and said to him, 'If anyone loves Me, he will keep My word; and My Father will love him, and We will come to him and make Our abode with him.*** *'He who does not love Me does not keep My words; and the word which you hear is not Mine, but the Father's who sent Me.'"*

Jesus is promising with His departure that He "will send another Helper that He may be with your forever, that is the Spirit of Truth." (14:16) During Pentecost this happened. The presence of the Holy Spirit arrived as promised with the sound of a mighty "violent wind from Heaven" and fire-like tongues of fire and they were all filled with the Holy Spirit". (Acts 2:1-4)

The presence of the Holy Spirit (Helper) that Jesus promised is here forever. So we all have the "same" Spirit. Jesus said the world cannot accept this truth or experience the Spirit because they cannot see or know Him. (This may remind you what many people say, "I can't see Him or prove His existence!) Walking in this world is walking in blindness or darkness. But walking in Christ is walking in the Light and we come to "know Him because He abides with you (us) and will be in you."

Let me begin with the first phrase, "He who has My commandments." This phrase is well understood that a person is in possession of the commandments of Jesus. Right? Well then, how does a person receive these commandments? By osmosis? Worship service? Sunday school? No to most, and yes to some extent to all.

> *Jesus' discipleship plan included practical field training, but we have to get out of the pews first.*

People come to grasp Christian doctrine on a small scale, but worship is not a discipling tool, it is a worship service. It is the time when folks come together to worship the Lord God. It is when we, the redeemed, sing praises unto His name, pray for others and ask Him to fill our lives with His presence.

> *Does your church's discipleship ministry resemble Jesus and the disciples?*

How did Jesus disciple His twelve? Let me tell you what He did not do. He did not set up a pulpit on a hill and place seats for lecture (preaching) on a bottom level. He didn't make three points and a poem or sing an offertory hymn with someone asking God's blessing on the money. He didn't have special music with a pipe organ, praise group or choir.

What Jesus did seems so passive it seems impossible to comprehend. He gathered the twelve in a small intimate group and He taught them. They might be sitting under a tree, beside the water or anywhere. He did not teach Christian theory, but Christian practice. Jesus taught them practical ways to minister and reach people. Believe it or not it is still effective in the 21st Century. He taught them to love everyone, to look within and around them and see what I call "jumping off points" to tell them the good news. Jumping off points are also known as Divine Appointments.

Jesus was addressing a group of Jews. (John 6) A gathered crowd sought a sign from Jesus as to His divinity and power. The crowd brought up the idea that God had provided bread (manna) from heaven while they were in the desert. Yet Jesus was trying to teach them the difference between bread of earth, which is temporary and bread sent by God in Him, an eternal source. The lesson Jesus taught was this:

> *"Jesus said to them, 'I am the bread of life; he who comes to Me will not hunger, and he who believes in Me will never thirst. But I said to you that you have seen Me, and yet do not believe. All that the Father gives Me will come to Me, and the one who comes to Me I will certainly not cast out. For I have*

come down from heaven, not to do My own will, but the will of Him who sent Me.'" (John 6:35–38)

Jesus taught (discipled) His followers in a practical field training too, not just hillside (classroom). The disciples saw Jesus healing the ill and raising the dead. They saw His compassion and ministry in the field and learned life-changing lessons. The people Jesus touched learned valuable lessons too.

This pastor prefers to follow this method of teaching, too. The churches I have pastored have had classroom work and field work. Men and women learn, like the disciples, how to pray, how to study Scriptures effectively, how to minister, how to witness and how to live successful lives in Christ. In addition, it is my conviction that we are not only building successful ministers and servants but mature and solid church leaders for tomorrow.

People must be taught. There is not an instantaneous diffusion of information given at salvation. We do discipleship because we are commanded to do so.

> *"And Jesus came up and spoke to them, saying, 'All authority has been given to Me in Heaven and on earth. Go therefore and make disciples of all the nations, baptizing them in the name of the Father and the Son and the Holy Spirit, teaching them to observe all that I commanded you; and lo, I am with you always, even to the end of the age.'"* (Matthew 28:18-20)

> **There is much more than walking the aisle and baptism there's obedience to Jesus command to disciple new believers**

Seemingly 20th Century churches began putting the emphasis on getting the person to walk the aisle, speaking to the pastor and telling Him, "I want to be saved." The church schedules a baptismal service; they're baptized and set loose, never to be taught how to follow Jesus or how to continue doing His work. When this life becomes hum-drum, these people often bail or when a new spiritual truth hits them they often pull back.

Let me impart a lesson I've learned from my study of Scriptures and people. If a church is not going to do discipleship, there's no need to do evangelism. These functions are the same and cannot be separated.

Jesus then turns from discipleship to practice. "He who has My commandments and keeps them…" Teaching people to follow Jesus is completely dependent upon the Light. The Holy Spirit must reveal the truth of God in the teaching process. Unless the Holy Spirit illuminates or reveals the truth, it can never be understood, received or applied to life. It is the Holy Spirit that gives conviction.

> *"But the Helper, the Holy Spirit, whom the Father will send in My name, He will teach you all things and bring to your remembrance all that I said to you."* (John 14:26)

> *"But when He, the Spirit of truth, comes, He will guide you into all the truth; for He will not speak on His own initiative, but whatever He hears, He will speak; and He will disclose to you what is to come. He will glorify Me, for He will take of Mine and will disclose it to you."* (John 16:13–14)

> *"but just as it is written, 'Things which eye has not seen and ear has not heard, And which have not entered the heart of man, All that God has prepared for those who love Him."* For to us God revealed them through the Spirit; for the Spirit searches all things, even the depths of God."* (1 Corinthians 2:9–10)

God's Revelation is not for information

All truth is a revelation from God. God takes those truths which are hidden and uses the Holy Spirit to unveil the truth so that you and I can begin to live with success, power and victory through Christ, Jesus. The Spirit of God is our guiding power in the Light. He illuminates the Word so that we may see it, understand it and apply it.

Have you ever heard someone say, "That was a powerful lesson (or sermon)?" My answer is what response to God do you need to make in response to God's Word today?

Our church has heard this statement over and over because as their shepherd they need to learn it.

- A revelation is not for information,
- A revelation is for transformation that leads to your participation
- And your participation gives glorification to God.

> *God's Revelation is for your transformation that leads to your participation and His glorification*

The core of this verse is not about head knowledge but on living out what one learns. Think of a child who is so curious, and they want to explore and know all they can. They are fascinated by those two small holes in the wall covered with a plastic plate. They want to know what's in there. Unfortunately, they can't see, taste or smell what's in an electrical outlet, but they can sure feel it. So, what does a parent do when they see their child reaching for something dangerous? They yell, "NO!" That's discipleship.

As we build on the next part of verse 21 "He who has My commandments and keeps them is the one who loves Me". The love of a follower (Christian) of Jesus is directly related to their obedience. Jesus set the example in His own life by being obedience to the Father, even unto death.

Calling Jesus Lord is comparable to calling Him, Master. Jesus is our Master. He led the way for us on earth. Those that followed Jesus were called "disciples" or learners. A disciple learned from the Master. Much the same parallel to a medical student learning from a doctor or any other trade or vocation. A trades person such as a carpenter, welder, plumber, concrete finisher, or roofer starts out as a "grunt". He or she grunts as he or she runs the errands and does the bidding of the master craftsman. We should be disciples or learners and allow Jesus to be the Master.

> *Love for Jesus is an emotional response, but more than that a response of doing what He taught*

"For I gave you an example that you also should do as I did to you. Truly, truly, I say to you, a slave is not greater than his master, nor is one who is sent greater than the one who sent him." (John 13:15–16)

Christian love is revealed, displayed, exhibited, or made apparent as a believer obeys the Lord's words. Maybe we need to define what love is. Have you caught yourself saying, "I love chocolate or something man-made? I have, and I have been working on not using the word "love" referring to stuff. Now I say, "I really like….." . Pecan pie was my true love of food.

Love can be used as a noun or a verb. Love is a deep admiration or an emotional response to a person. For example, I love my kids. I love my wife. I love my parents. I love our pastor. Too many times do not see love as a deep concern for a person or their welfare.

Love of Jesus is an affectionate emotional response for the sacrifice He made to reconcile you and me, a sinner, to a Holy God. This love also shows a concern for Jesus' welfare. I know what can we do to enhance the life of Jesus? Share Him with the Lost! Be concerned for His Kingdom by promoting it. Love is sacrificial. I am not speaking of burned offerings but giving up something that was once important. One might want to give up old habits, old friends, and old hang-outs for their newly redeemed life. In the grand scheme of life, these are not a sacrifice. The list is endless of possibilities.

Love for Jesus is best exhibited by doing what He has taught. I know you are going to say, "I fail from time to time." Well, you are human. I fail. Every person with breath in their body has failed. But the goal or aim is to correct those failings with obedience. But a continued lifestyle of disobedience isn't an accident. It's unredeemed, untransformed life walking in darkness.

Healthy love is a growing love. Have you ever noticed you love your spouse differently than when you first married? One begins to accept the other's inadequacies and flaws. What was once a source of argument becomes a settled peace. Love matures. The Apostle Paul described love:

> *"'For this, 'You shall not commit adultery, You shall not murder, You shall not steal, You shall not covet, and if there is any other commandment, it is summed up in this saying, 'You shall love your neighbor as yourself.' Love does no wrong to a neighbor; therefore, love is the fulfillment of the law.'"* (Romans 13:9–10)

> *"'Love is patient, love is kind and is not jealous; love does not brag and is not arrogant, does not act unbecomingly; it does not seek its own, is not provoked, does not take into account a wrong suffered, does not rejoice in unrighteousness, but rejoices with the truth; bears all things, believes all things, hopes all things, endures all things. Love never fails; But now faith, hope, love, abide these three; but the greatest of these is love.'"* (1 Corinthians 13:4- 8; 13)

There are many passages within the Gospel where Jesus directly addressed obedience. Now, we need to look at the benefits of obedience. Whenever we encounter a passage of Scripture, whether in our private reading, a Bible-study class or a sermon, we must ask ourselves, "What do I need to do in response to this passage. The Scriptures are not there for entertainment, but each on has an application that the hearer or reader must respond to the passage in order to be obedient.

Obedience is simply, doing what the Word of God reveals. Look at the passage above in Romans 13:9-10. The passage states, *"You shall love your neighbor as yourself."* What does it mean and how can you be obedience. (By the way, this is a commandment, equal with all others.)

It was first given to Israel in the Exodus experience in Leviticus 19:18. This passage was a quote from Jesus in Matthew 19:19;

22:39; Romans 13:9; Galatians 5:14 and James 2:8. Mark and Luke included this passage in their Gospels. Repeated so many times one has to ask, "Is it important?" Yes it is!

To begin, in Matthew 22:37-38 Jesus gives us a command that goes back to the law given in the desert on the Exodus journey, *"And He said to him, 'You shall love the Lord your God with all your heart, and with all your soul, and with all your mind. This is the great and foremost commandment."* This love is aimed directly at God, Himself in which there are never anything or anyone more important than one's relationship to God. The believer is to love Him with everything above everything.

The second commandment of "love your neighbor as yourself" is built upon the first. One cannot fulfill the first commandment without fulfilling the second commandment. It is also crucial to understand that if you cannot love your neighbor as yourself, you cannot possibly love God. The Epistle of James addresses this love in many ways, but always within the context of caring for others.

Love is a characteristic of God. "God is love." (1 John 3:8) Many people know John 3:16, *"For God so loved the world, that He gave His only begotten Son, that whoever believes in Him shall not perish, but have eternal life.* This verse is a key truth in all the Gospels, because it was God's love that was responsible for Jesus' birth, ministry, death, burial and resurrection.

The love of God is given to every genuine believer at salvation. It is who a redeemed believer is because we contain the Spirit of the Living God. Love is natural in the Spirit, but foreign in the unredeemed world.

If you love the Lord your God with all of your heart, soul and your mind you will discover the deepest and most satisfying love that has ever existed. Then, all other relationships will be put into to proper perspective and built upon the Truth of God.

Love is transforming

8 UNDERSTANDING GOD'S LOVE FOR US

"Jesus answered and said to him, 'If anyone loves Me, he will keep My word; and My Father will love him, and We will come to him and make Our home with him.'" (John 14:23)

When Jesus said, "If anyone loves Me," He gave three beautifully warming, compelling and loving truths of why people, lost or redeemed, need to walk in the light: The Father's love - we will come to him and we will make our (abode in some translations) home with him. If you think these are weak reasons consider this: billions of people of every culture and tongue follow a religion, which is trying to find a god. Often, they search for, read books about and try out these religions, but most of the time they become thoroughly confused and hostile towards "religion".

Americans have probably the greatest need of the presence of the Living God in their lives of the whole planet. Why? Because so many people are proud they walk in darkness and do not want God. A tremendous amount of people walk in the shadows of God, neither in the light nor the darkness. These people may think their relationship with Almighty God is "alright" because they've walked the aisle, been baptized and have their name on the church roll. The sad truth about the "Shadow Walkers" is more than likely they are lost and have a false security because of the external factors of baptism and church membership.

Our American society's ills and even apathy for the suffering and lost people are additional proof we are in frantic need of the Living God to be able to live in our lives. We need His presence and His power, if we are to achieve spiritual victory. This power is only available if we walk in His Light.

1. Love of God – "If anyone loves Me" (John 14:23 excerpt)

Love for ourselves, others and God begins with God loving us. God is love. (1 John 4:8 and 4:16) We may attempt to describe God in many ways, terms and phrases, but our description of God is incomplete. God's character or His inner-most nature is love. Personally, I wonder if a lot of people comprehend His Divine love is so strong that He desires a relationship with His creation, us. In this relationship God's deepest desire is that we return the love given to us back to Him.

Which is easier to love or to hate? Some people have a tendency to be hyper-critical of others. I wonder if some people have a need to elevate themselves at the expense of others? There are plenty of people, including ministers that I do not agree with, but to hate – that's out of the question. Truly there may be people we had rather not be near, but God still expects us to love them.

We are witnessing an attitude in the early decade of the 21st Century with liberals verses conservatives, ideologies verses ideologies and even theologies at the center of the dispute, driving wedges within the society, families and churches. There is plenty of proof within the actions and words of people to say, "I have to be right and you are wrong!" Sometimes it appears people are at some interdimensional war with each other.

You may say I am naive and have an idealistic view, but this is the view of God Almighty according to His Word. Individuals are different. We have different likes and dislikes, beliefs, strengths, and abilities. We should be driven by love, not our differences or expressing our differences in such negative ways. This attitude of division is common among those who do not walk in the Light of God. The need to elevate one's self above another is a history-long certainty.

Recorded history has given us too many examples not to accept this fact. In Genesis 4:1-9, Cain killed his brother Abel because of

Cain's jealousy over God's acceptance of Abel's offering. In Genesis 37:3 one can see that Israel (later known as Jacob) loved his son Joseph more than the other children. Joseph had a dream about how his brothers would bow before him and they hated Joseph even more because of his dream. (Genesis 37:5) Eventually his brothers would sell him into bondage in Egypt and that's how the Hebrews became the Egyptian slaves. By the way, Joseph's brothers did bow before him in Egypt. Even the Egyptians became fearful of the quickly multiplying population of the Hebrews fearing they would overthrow Egypt. That's why Egypt put such hard labor upon the Hebrews. They believed if we work them to death they won't have the energy to have children. (Exodus 1:7-15 and further)

History also shows us other examples of one people focusing upon or conquering other people because of their beliefs. The Jews of the First Century (Jesus' day) hated the Samaritans, a half-bred Jew. They would walk around Samaria to travel to the other side of the nation. The Crusaders of the 11th – 13th Centuries warred against the Muslims that had taken over the Holy Land. There is a modern-day rivalry between Catholics and Evangelicals and other "so-called" Christian groups verses the church. There is the example of Adolf Hitler, North Korea verses South Korea as conquerors for an increase in their power or for economic reasons. Many cannot forget the struggle between the Communist country U.S.S.R. (Russia) and the Western nations of the United States, Great Brittan and France because of the Western idea of capitalism and freedom.

We cannot leave America out. What about the slavery of the centuries leading up to the Civil War? Both sides had their reasons and I'm not here to debate this issue, but the fact remains there were two completely opposing ideologies about this way of life. Both sides, the North (Yankees) and the South (Rebels) lost tremendous numbers of people. According to the data of American Battlefield Trust, nearly 620,000 people lost their lives in the bloody conflict with possibilities perhaps as high as 850,000. Also, according to their website (www.battlefields.org) the number of Americans killed in World Wars I and II amounted to 521,000.

Love, many times, doesn't show in our interpersonal and international struggles. The opposite appears to be the rule many times. What does God's Word say about love? Since God is love and out of this love He created us to walk in a relationship of love with Him and our fellow man, we must accept His view.

> **God will never compete for our love**

Anyone who reads through the Gospels should see that Jesus walked in the love of God. His entire ministry on earth was spent loving and ministering to people. Jesus spent time with people. He lovingly taught and corrected their wayward lives from God. Jesus cared for the hurts and needs of the people. His love for humanity was and is still today His driving motive.

The First Epistle of John (1 John) has 226 verses teaching about God loving us and how we should return His love and express it in our relationships to others. I have this temptation to call 1 John the Epistle of Love. Look at the following passages about the subject of love.

> *Do not love the world nor the things in the world. If anyone loves the world, the love of the Father is not in him. For all that is in the world, the lust of the flesh and the lust of the eyes and the boastful pride of life, is not from the Father, but is from the world. The world is passing away, and also its lusts; but the one who does the will of God lives forever."* (1 John 2:15–17)

You may notice God does not want to compete for our love. The passage above gives us a great truth that everyone should pay special attention to understand and follow. Love of the world translates the things of this temporary existence on earth. The Apostle John included the lust. This word means a deep, longing desire. One can lust or have a deep, longing desire after power, wealth, position, sexual intimacy, fame, or material possessions. This basically means one spends a great deal of their wakeful time thinking or planning how they can achieve their goals. John warned the people this attitude was not from God. If it isn't from God then it has to be from the Devil, tempting a person away from God. Verse 17 tells us that all these things are temporary, but the presence of God in one's life is eternal. He finishes his statement by saying, "but the one who does the will of God lives forever." Would you rather have a pleasure for a brief moment in time or for all eternity?

One's love for God transforms one's attitude about others. God's love, living in us, gives us the same heart, mind and concern for everyone around us, but more especially those who are born-again, co-existing in the Spirit of God. Our treatment, care and concern for our fellow believers should be a model for the rest of the world. Here the Apostle John indicates that a person walking in the Light of God's love does not walk in darkness or even the shadow of darkness and there is nothing there to make the person stumble (sin). But should someone's heart contain hate for a brother, then he or she is walking in darkness (sin, the absence of God) and cannot make sense of his direction because the darkness (Satan) has blinded his or her eyes against the truth and light of God.

> *"The one who loves his brother abides in the Light and there is no cause for stumbling in him. But the one who hates his brother is in the darkness and walks in the darkness and does not know where he is going because the darkness has blinded his eyes."* (1 John 2:10–11)

John continues his thought in the next chapter of his epistle. Here the difference between those walking in the light and those walking in darkness. John used Cain and Able of Genesis 4 as an example.

Many people of the 21st Century believe they are right before God as long as they go to church, avoid places like bars and sexually explicit movies, have a fake smile or say the right words and avoid the wrong words. Throughout Scriptures the true emphasis of righteous is doing the right thing in the eyes of the Lord. John stated a plain truth, "who does not practice righteousness is not of God, nor the one who does not love his brother." Do not judge your life according to what you think about your life, but in light of God's Holy Word. If you are a child of God and genuinely love Him you will live in the love of others. He wrote in the next two sets of verses:

> *"By this the children of God and the children of the devil are obvious: anyone who does not practice righteousness is not of God, nor the one who does not love his brother. For this is the message which you have heard from the beginning, that we should love one another; not as Cain, who was of the evil one and slew his brother. And for what reason did he slay him? Because his deeds were evil, and his brothers' were righteous."* (1 John 3:10–12)

> *"But whoever has the world's goods, and sees his brother in need and closes his heart against him, how does the love of God abide in him? Little children, let us not love with word or with tongue, but in deed (actions) and truth."* (1 John 3:17–18)

God wants us to love Him, not for what He does for us, but because of whom He is. He is the Holy One who created the world around you to give you life and the necessities of life. He has given us everything we need, such as jobs, homes, food to eat, transportation, breath, heartbeat, others to love us and help us through life. The most valuable gift He has given to us is His Son, Jesus. He was the substitutionary payment for the penalty of our sin problem.

> *How do you demonstrate your love for your spouse or children?*

Our obedience to the person and Word of God is dependent upon our love for Him. Let me ask you a question, "How do you ultimately demonstrate your love to your spouse, children, parents or friends?" Deeds are one good way to demonstrate one's love for another. Most people want to demonstrate their love to their family through physical contact of a hug, a kiss, holding hands or spousal intimacy. But deeds can also include a husband cooking supper for a tired wife after her long difficult day at work or buying her a flower (many dozens if he's messed up and is threatened with sleeping on the couch). Deeds also include having a daddy or mommy day with a child and making your child feel like he or she is the center of your universe.

The second way a person demonstrates their love for their family and friends is by being there for them. A person who loves another is there when the person is down, depressed, lonely, or hurting. They may not be able to achieve real, tangible outcomes which is beside the point. Simply being there and showing your love for another is more powerful than any spoken words. Many times when I do hospital or funeral home visits, I do not say much of anything except, "I am here for you. I love you and care for you" and do more listening than speaking.

While spending 70 days awaiting my heart transplant there was a time when I was basically alone. About 5 weeks prior to the end of school is when I was admitted for advanced heart failure. My wife was still having to finish out her school year and this meant I was alone in an isolated ICU without my friends or loved ones. There were times when I wondered how much longer would I have to withstand this torture? When Karen was able to come to the hospital, I felt complete! She replaced my loneliness with her presence. Karen made a sacrifice of love for me at the expense of her own energy level or other things she needed to do.

How has God demonstrated His love for us? We can find the answers throughout the New Testament. God showed His love for us long before we ever realized we needed Him. Look at the following passages:

> *"God demonstrates His own love toward us, in that while we were yet sinners, Christ died for us."* (Romans 5:8)

> *"For God so loved the world that He gave His only begotten Son, that whoever believes in Him shall not perish, but have eternal life. For God did not send the Son into the world to judge the world, but that the world might be saved through Him. He who believes in Him is not judged; he who does not believe has been judged already, because he has not believed in the name of the only begotten Son of God."* (John 3:16–18)

The love of God is demonstrated to His people in His Word from Genesis 1:1 to the back cover of your Bible. God's love for you is not dependent upon who you are, what you do or do not do. God's love is not about you jumping through hoops, building a hospital or volunteering at a local charity. It is there because God is love (1 John 4:8).

One day John 3:16 came to mind because so many people go around quoting it. The Holy Spirit kept drawing me to the first phrase, "For God so loved the world." The Greek noun here is kosmos or universe, but it means the people who dwell on earth. The word intrigued me and peaked my curiosity to study the Word of God on this subject more.

God loves all the people, but especially those who are His, loved? God loves us all, no exclusions. Some people have a problem with that and I wonder if it is because they want to be Exclusionist or Elitist? I don't have that answer, but after a great deal of prayer and meditation on this idea I sensed this: the evilest people God loves, too.

God created us out of a desire to have a person to love and someone, by free choice, to love Him back. We live under God in a free choice state, not as a bunch of robots which He controls with a huge remote control from heaven. If that were the case – can you imagine how many times He would feel like his remote-control batteries were dead because He's trying to control us and we're not responding.

I was tempted to say, "OK, God loves those who are born-again. Yes, He does for His Word states that but it's much more. He loves everyone. My weak reasoning revealed to me that God even loved the most detestable man of the 20th Century, Adolph Hitler, who was responsible for millions of deaths in World War II, even over 6 million of God's chosen people, the Jews.

So, what is unique about God's love for all of His creation, mankind? The answer is His loving provisions. He wants to provide for His creations. After all He created us all. Look at Adam and Even in the Garden. God told them (Genesis 2) they may eat the fruit of any tree but warned them not to eat of the fruit of the Tree of Knowledge of Good and Evil. God told them that if they ate that fruit they would know good and evil. In Genesis 3:6, Eve saw the fruit would make her wise and she ate the fruit and gave is also to Adam. After they ate the forbidden fruit they realized their nakedness and became ashamed. Truly their eyes were opened, but to a truth they didn't want to see. So the first recording of God's love was banishment from the Garden with "flaming swords" guarding the entrance to prevent them from re-entering the Garden and eating of the Tree of Life. Many Bible scholars believe that had Adam and Eve been able to eat of this tree after falling into sin they would be condemned, and so would all of humanity, to be doomed to a life of sin without redemption. So, while God's action may on the surface appear to be harsh, it was a loving act.

Love is caring. Parents usually care for their children and raise them to become fully independent and self-functioning. They love their children by protecting them. Parents love their children by feeding them and giving their little ones warm clothes and take care of them when they are sick. I see this and understand this from the Scriptures as God's loving care for you and me.

> **Love is caring**

God loves us and wants to care for us in many ways like human parents do their children but on a deeper level. He has unimaginable power and exists outside of the limitations of time. When our children become gravely ill, we can only take them to doctors and many times the doctors can only make them comfortable or try to find something to get rid of the illness or disease. But the Lord God can heal them. This example is repeated many times in the New Testament through Jesus. The Gospels are filled with the fact that people had faith in Jesus' healing ability and sought Him out for deliverance from the disease.

Today we still see people that are miraculously healed. God still "cares" for people and wants them and the world to know how much He loves them. Sometimes healings come in restored relationships, sometimes in physical healings and other times in emotional healings.

Many people experience the loving provisions of God's care through other various means like finding a home or an auto, too. In 2001 my vehicle was falling apart, and we committed our need through prayer. We did the normal looking and talking to auto dealers and one day discovered a small pickup that matched our needs perfectly. Yeah, I know, I'm talking about a material need. But I still use that small truck as primary transportation. I often thank the Heavenly Father for His guidance for this nearly trouble-free truck. This is only one example we've experienced, but I have discovered God's provisions in many areas of our life.

As a word of testimony, I have been the recipient of God's unbelievable love. When I was 33 years old, I had my first heart attack. I was following in the footsteps of my mother and her father. Over the next twenty years, I would have seven more heart attacks. Twice I had to have by-pass surgery after an attack. One day my cardiologist told me my heart was too weak and he would have to install a pacemaker to guard against a sudden run-away heart rate that would kill me. I lived with the pacemaker for five years until the heart had become so weak that I had to live in ICU and await a match for transplant. Then on July 5th, the doctor came to my room and said, "We have you a heart. You will be taken to surgery tomorrow for transplant. So, July 6th became my new birth day.

God has given me a new life and I celebrate it minute by minute. Some might say, "Oh, transplants are a common place, everyday thing." They aren't! God has to provide an exact biological match between donor and recipient. Not every donor can be used because of various reasons. Then there is the organ rejection possibility. The organ recipient is having a foreign object placed in their body and the body wants to get rid of the foreign object. So, anti-rejections medications must be taken. Not everyone lives.

I cannot explain why God chose me. But this I know – I was never alone in my bed before or after transplant. He was there with me, holding my hand, stroking my brow, speaking into my ear how much He loved me. There were days my spirit was heavy and I wondered if I were doing the right thing. Sometimes I questioned, "How much longer?" The loving Lord would send someone by my room that encouraged me beyond description.

I didn't receive this organ because of my personal holiness. The heart was a gift from God because of His great love for me. Now I am the caretaker of someone else's heart. My wife and I were given the opportunity to travel and meet the family of my heart. They were deeply hurting because their son, my donor, was shot to death and they were still mourning their loss plus the agony of his murderer who had not been tried yet. We had the occasion to love on the parents and their family and to allow them to hear the heart of their beloved son beating in my heart. God gave me a new family that I love as my own and care for deeply.

God is love! (I John 4:8) Would you be willing to surrender to the undeserved love of God?

We have a foundation for love being from God. Now we must look at the Word of God in relationship to "if anyone loves Me." Jesus said, "If anyone loves me, he will keep My Word."

2 - The people's loving response – "If anyone loves Me, he will keep My word"

> *"By this we know that we have come to know Him, if we keep His commandments. The one who says, "I have come to know Him," and does not keep His commandments, is a liar, and the truth is not in him; but whoever keeps His word, in him the love of God has truly been perfected. By this we know that we are in Him:* (1 John 2:3–5)

Many people think God has too many rules and regulations to be followed. They express a heavy burden or load carrying around this responsibility. Yet Jesus said, *"Come to Me, all who are weary and heavy-laden, and I will give you rest. Take My yoke upon you and learn from Me, for I am gentle and humble in heart, and YOU WILL FIND REST FOR YOUR SOULS. For My yoke is easy and My burden is light."* (Matthew 11:28–30) Remember this is God in the flesh, (Jesus) speaking.

> **God is about Him loving us and our love returned, not rule keeping**

God cannot tell a lie. The character of God makes Him unable and therefore all from God is spoken in love and truth. He used the yoke which is a wooden harness connecting two animals. Here Jesus is telling us our connection (relationship) to Him is not difficult and the load isn't heavy, but rather all who take this yoke can find rest for our souls.

Personally, I have never found following Jesus to be filled with rules and regulations. He never forces a person to believe or do something. When Jesus said, "my yoke is easy and my burden is light" He means that it isn't a life filled with troublesome rules. Too often man makes up the rules. Rather following Jesus is easy, but one must open their heart and mind to follow Him wherever He leads.

Let me bear witness to the truth of following Him. Many years ago, I was a corporate banker who loved my job. I truly thought I'd be doing this the rest of my life. Circumstance changed when F.D.I.C. came into our bank and found the bank President made many questionable and sometimes illegal loans. This was a time in which the federal regulators were lowering the hammer on banks and savings and loans. The F.D.I.C. took possession of the bank and my services were no longer needed. I was unemployed.

My family had become accustomed to this income. Life was extraordinarily tough without it. My wife and I had several jobs just to put groceries on the table. She would go to work at a fast-food place after her full-time job. I had four different part-time jobs. God had provided for us income, not luxurious, but ample.

The flexible schedule allowed me to be more involved in our church's youth ministry. Despite the difficulties of job, I found deep joy helping the youth discover the joy of following the Lord, themselves. This opportunity caused me to learn more about the Lord and discover more of His deeper truths and love for me. As a result, I sensed a change of mind from banking to ministry. The Holy Spirit began to slowly work and change my priorities to the

Person of God. One Sunday morning during the invitation time, I told our pastor that I sensed the Lord calling me into ministry. In Wikipedia under the word surprise is a picture of our pastor. He was shocked! He wasn't as shocked as my wife, who told me, "She married a banker not a preacher!"

My wife sought out pastoral counseling because she couldn't understand how or why this happened. Our pastor advised Karen to wait and see what God does. He told her if God was in this decision, nothing could stop it, but if He wasn't, nothing could bring this to reality. She agreed, and we prayed about this for two years until both found peace and were of one mind.

It has been my experience in life as well as observing others that the love for God develops slowly once it registers in our minds and hearts. The Lord never forced me to do anything about this feeling, but I felt a strong desire to follow through with what I felt. The Holy Spirit began to give me a burning desire to know the Father more and how I might obediently follow Him. The more time I spent studying His Word and in prayer the more I wanted to know and follow Him.

Then, one day a small rural country church asked me to preach for them. I did and a few days later they called and asked if I'd like to be their pastor. I cannot tell you what went through my mind, but I knew I didn't know anything and felt so inadequate and ill-prepared. I accepted the pastorate and found the more sermon preparation I did the more I begin to grow.

To shorten the story, I began part-time seminary classes at a church one evening a week. This was exactly what I needed. After a year and one half I realized I need more, faster. If you want to know how God works, I asked Karen to pray about moving to New Orleans, Louisiana to go fulltime to seminary. The definition of crazy is "a Texan moving to Louisiana." There's nothing wrong with

Louisiana, but to move away from home, family and friends and not have a job! We did, and the Father blessed this time and set in motion my deepening desire to know and experience Him. He began with a spark of love He put in my and grew that spark to a roaring inferno.

In the Great Commission (Matthew 28:18-20) Jesus gave a command to the disciples that applies to every Christian today. He said, "And Jesus came up and spoke to them, saying, *'All authority has been given to Me in heaven and on earth. Go therefore and make disciples of all the nations, baptizing them in the name of the Father and the Son and the Holy Spirit, teaching them to observe all that I commanded you; and lo, I am with you always, even to the end of the age.'*

The Great Commission *is not a suggestion*

This passage goes beyond commandments into the basic teachings of Jesus. A large part of the Gospels are devoted to Jesus' teaching. While the Great Commission (above) addresses the idea of making disciples, the way disciples are made is by teaching the person all that Jesus taught within the New Testament Scriptures. Jesus used parables, which are stories with a lesson. He used visual demonstrations, such as healing people who had lifetimes of ailments, driving out demons from possessed people, raising the dead (Lazarus) in John 11:14 and public teaching for all to hear, such as the Sermon on the Mount. I suggest you read the Gospels and allow the Holy Spirit to fill you with the truth of this idea of Jesus' teachings.

Jesus was not teaching a bunch of rules and regulations. Rules are such rigid ideas, but rather Jesus taught the truths of God for victorious and successful living. If one wants to live in the victory of the Resurrection of Jesus, one must be willing to be flexible in their own life rather than rigidly saying, "I want to live life my way." God will allow you to live life your way, but that tends to be selfish in its intent. Rather He wants you and me to live according to His will, His purposes for our lives and His ways. After all, He is the One who created us.

Let me take the idea of living according to the Creator's wishes a bit further. Men are well known for being know-it-alls. We buy kids swings and throw away the assembly instructions. Then when something comes out twisted we scratch our head, throw a wrench or two and finally when we can't figure it out, we ask our wives. Their first words are, "Where are the instructions?" If one goes by the instructions in the first place one doesn't get as frustrated as one does without them. There are other pluses – our wives don't see us as a less than perfect man she married, and the kids don't learn our tendencies.

How can you and I love God, by obeying His Word? First, I recommend a good Bible translation. I have my favorite, but each person must find that translation that they can understand. Some people prefer the King James Translation, others the New International Version and one more that is highly recommended, the New King James. There are several modern translations that are highly accurate to the original manuscripts, but comprehension is the important factor. Personally, I prefer the New American Standard which I use almost exclusively because it is a fairly precise translation from the original Greek.

Whatever translation you chose, read it. Keep it with you at all times and even carry it with you to work. I recommend this because I have found times I sensed the Holy Spirit speaking to me and I need to jot down that thought when I get home, if I haven't gotten busy and forgot it. If you find yourself with some idle time, read. Some pastors, churches and Christians promote reading through your Bible in a year. That is a good idea when you first get started, but after the first time, read it for inspiration. The idea is reading the Word of God for the Spirit of God to speak to you and transform your mind, heart and life. Reading at a break-neck speed will not accomplish this goal.

There are times, as I am reading the Word of God, that the Holy Spirit draws me to a verse or word. As often as this happens, I begin to study that passage deeply with intensity and over time to learn the message and truth God has for me. The idea is to prayerfully discover what God is trying to tell you. What truth is He wanting you to take into your heart and mind.

When I am preaching or teaching, I will bring this biblical truth to light for the people and I want you to see it too. A sermon, (Sunday School or Bible Study) is not for information. The Word of God is your inspiration. The biblical word "inspiration" means breathed into. God breathes life and meaning into His Word. The Lord God inspires or breathes life into His Word through the Holy Spirit that resides in those who love Jesus. Without the presence of the Holy Spirit or if our life is full of unrepented sin we will read and reread a passage and say, "I can't understand this!" If this happens, pray. Ask God for the truth of this passage and He will give it to you. Be warned, when He shows it, respond to it immediately without hesitation.

The Apostle Paul was teaching young Pastor Timothy a valuable lesson. He said, *"All Scripture is inspired by God and profitable for teaching, for reproof, for correction, for training in righteousness; so that the man of God may be adequate, equipped for every good work."* (2 Timothy 3:16–17) It is God who gives the Word life.

There is another term I would like to pass on, that's revelation. There is a book by this name, but the idea is even in the book that John had received a revelation from God. The subject of "end times" brings a lot of discussion, arguments and speculation. God wanted to give a glimpse of the "end of time" for the benefit of the churches. So, God revealed pieces of His plan to John to communicate to the churches. Some say the book of Revelation is a book of doom and gloom. I am sure this attitude is based upon one's walk in Christ more than anything, but I see it as a book of hope. When will suffering end? What is Heaven like?

Many people have ordinary, everyday revelations that do not necessarily have anything to do with a message from God. A revelation could be to add an ingredient in a recipe that would make the texture or taste better. One might be searching for their car keys and finally think, "Ah, hah!" These are not life-changing revelations in most cases. A revelation refers to something once hidden and now revealed. I am referring to Scripture as one is reading or a truth popping out to you from the Scriptures.

When God inspires you or reveals His truth to you, it is never for information, it is for a transformation. The Lord God wants to transform you more into the image of His Son, Jesus. That is why He drew you to that verse in the first place. The Word of God will transform a person, who has accepted the idea that they want to be more like Jesus and welcome the transformation.

> *If you dislike change you won't like following Jesus or Heaven!*

We are all being transformed. When I was 30, I had dark hair. Now I don't! When I was 30 I needed a slight eyeglasses prescription and now I need bifocals. Life is in a constant mode of change. Why shouldn't our spiritual lives be constantly changing?

Some people say, "I hate change!" Some changes I agree with wholeheartedly. I dislike some changes in technology because it requires a complete relearning. Presently many churches are going through changes in the choice of music, ministry or even staff.

There is an old saying is, "Change is unavoidable." If one is to walk in the Light, one must be willing to change as the Holy Spirit leads. Many people and churches are living in the "good ole days" and prefer to live in yesterday. I recognize this when I hear someone say, "Back in the _____ (decades past) we use to have ____ amount of people in worship and now we're slowly dying."

There's a solid reason why this is happening. Our world has changed and how we go about reaching people for Christ must also change. People are different. Their problems are different. Their needs are different. We no longer live in an Ozzie and Harriet or Leave it to Beaver society where everything is rosy. We live in a day where shootings in public schools happen way too often. Divorce has soared over the past three decades and many families are now headed by moms without dads or they are living with the blending of more than one family. Job stability has gone out of the window. You name it, it has changed.

Only one organization has resisted change and is paying a heavy price – the church. Instead of being the salt and light of the world (Matthew 5:13), we are either in danger of becoming or already become the sugar and neon of the world. There is a saying that is capturing the hearts and minds of church leaders today and it is, "The definition of insanity is doing the same thing over and over again and expecting different results." (Unknown author) Or, you might say, "If you continue doing the same old things that didn't work then you cannot expect different results now."

Jesus said, "You are the salt and light of the world. (Matthew 5:13) His reference is two-fold. First, Salt was valuable in that day. It was used as a currency. That's where the phrase "worth the weight in salt" originates. Salt flavors but more importantly preserves. Meat was preserved for many millennials by using salt as a covering for fresh, uncooked meat to preserve it. The application for this church is this: the saved children of God, through Christ Jesus is to serve as a preservative for society. We, as the preservative, are to influence our societies in a way that prevents it from spoiling from unrighteousness or sin. In other words, we are to be a positive influence in the world leading individuals to the "preserved" state or salvation for eternity in Christ, Jesus.

The "light" is similar to Jesus' teaching about the salt. Light shows the safe path to walk and prevents accidents by tripping or falling off a cliff. More significantly, "light" is reference to Jesus as the Light and we are commanded by Jesus to be His voice on earth and to lead people, as witnesses, to the saving knowledge of God. We, as followers of Jesus, are to show the way to Jesus and to be beacons of light ourselves.

Churches and some leaders recognize times have changed and so must our efforts if we are going to reach people for Christ. But, they continue to do the same old things and wonder, why people aren't attracted to their churches. The people and the leadership may say, "I see the problems and hear what help others offer to help but despite many encouragements to church leaderships, from many sources, they seem to ignore it. Why? Possibly because some church leaders are stuck in the past and they're afraid of change themselves because maybe they fear their congregation or being caught without the answers themselves. There is another possibility – there is no God-given vision because either the pastor or the church or both are not truly walking in the Light.

Light represents Christ's presence in our lives. In the world of commerce, the head of an organization communicates with his or her workers their plans and actions. The same is true of Jesus and His church. We have the one Holy Spirit, the Spirit of the Living God living in us to communicate both ways. Christ naturally communicates with His children and His church to guide us in the plans He has, and actions we must take.

Many people will be tempted to say, "Well God never changes!"

True, or "The Gospel never changes!" They are right, but even Jesus brought change to His day. The Pharisees and Scribes were challenged when Jesus taught, preached and ministered. I would be willing to say Jesus' audience heard from these groups of leaders the very same thing we hear mumbled in churches today, "We'll we ain't never done it that way before!" That is the kicker. The <u>church has to change</u> the way it ministers to their community to reach them for Christ.

The largest group of people in the United States today are the Millennials. The largest group has the smallest representation within churches. According to current research only 5% are believers. Millennials will not grasp the spiritual mentality of previous generations. They can be more dedicated to Christ, but they do not typically see the life of Jesus within the church. Jesus loved people and went to them. Most churches do not. Jesus didn't spend a huge amount on fancy buildings, too often we do. Millennials want to see more of the "sacred offering" going to ministry within their community and impacting people at home. This is quite a scratchy point for the Baby-boomers and older.

But, avoiding spiritual changes is life-threatening. It is sin either for the corporate church or the individual. Once I heard a pastor say, "You cannot stay where you are and go with God." Too often we think we know where to go and once we've come up with a plan then we ask God to bless it. This is putting the proverbial cart in front of the horse. Neither a person nor a church should go anywhere until they have clearly heard from God as to the specifics and details.

> *Avoiding spiritual changes is life-threatening*

In desperation churches often develop strategies to minister or evangelize their community. When you ask what God has specifically said to them their answer is, "Ah, ah, ah!" When their plans fail they often assume many things which most are probably wrong. What is most probably the right answer is that they never asked God for direction in the first place.

Now let me address a popular, though worldly point, "How can someone love another whom one hasn't seen?" Is it possible for me to love someone in India living in the remote North? Love a person that I haven't seen? This may be where many Christians get hung up on "love your neighbor". This is also a question raised throughout time about God. God has been known throughout history as the invisible God.

The Apostle Paul described to the church at Colossae what Jesus had accomplished for us all by writing,

> *"For He rescued us from the domain of darkness and transferred us to the kingdom of His beloved Son, in whom we have redemption, the forgiveness of sins. He is the image of the <u>invisible</u> God, the firstborn of all creation. For by Him all things were created, both in the heavens and on earth, visible and <u>invisible</u>, whether thrones or dominions or rulers or authorities - all things have been created through Him and for Him. He is before all things, and in Him all things hold together. He is also head of the body, the church; and He is the beginning, the firstborn from the dead, so that He Himself will come to have first place in everything. For it was the Father's good pleasure for all the fullness to dwell in Him, and through Him to reconcile all things to Himself, having made peace through the blood of His cross; through Him, I say,*

whether things on earth or things in heaven." (Colossians 1:13–20)

Notice, twice Paul refers to God with the word "invisible". In verse 15, Paul refers to Jesus as the Son of the invisible God. We highly advanced people of the 21st Century appear to have been influenced by scientist more than we can imagine. Scientists want proof. They want to be able to measure or quantify something. My study of science as an early college major was to take a theory, study it, measure it, observe it and form an opinion based upon facts that are observable. One cannot prove what one cannot see, smell, hear, or measure. So, as a result many people cannot believe who haven't seen. Yet the Apostle Peter wrote:

"In this you greatly rejoice, even though now for a little while, if necessary, you have been distressed by various trials, so that the proof of your faith, being more precious than gold which is perishable, even though tested by fire, may be found to result in praise and glory and honor at the revelation of Jesus Christ; and though you have not seen Him, you love Him, and though you do not see Him now, but believe in Him, you greatly rejoice with joy inexpressible and full of glory, obtaining as the outcome of your faith the salvation of your souls." (1 Peter 1:6–12)

The writer of Romans challenges us from the standpoint of proof verses faith. He wrote:

"For the wrath of God is revealed from heaven against all ungodliness and unrighteousness of men who suppress the truth in unrighteousness, because that which is known about God is evident within them; for God made it evident to them. For since the creation of the world His invisible attributes, His eternal power and divine nature, have been clearly seen, being understood through what has been made, so that they are

without excuse. For even though they knew God, they did not honor Him as God or give thanks, but they became futile in their speculations, and their foolish heart was darkened." (Romans 1:18–21)

Jesus taught us in the Great Commandment to love our neighbor.

"And He said to him, 'You shall love the Lord your God with all your heart, and with all your soul, and with all your mind. This is the great and foremost commandment. The second is like it, 'You shall love your neighbor as yourself. On these two commandments depend the whole Law and the Prophets.'" (Matthew 22:37–40)

Usually people have a natural tendency to love themselves in very healthy ways. We know we need food, so we go to the grocery store or raise our food and then eat it. We may sense our bodies going hay-wire and go to the doctor. When it is cold we put on warmer clothes to protect us. Loving ourselves means we seek to provide the necessities for ourselves.

Sometimes we see our society demonstrate an absence of love for one's self through self-indulgence and addictions. This does not mean these people are bad people, but they have no significant desire to live in a way that promotes their own well-being.

There are many ways to see our God, Creator and Savior. Romans 1:20 indicates that the Heavenly Father with His invisible attributes, His eternal power and divine nature have been clearly seen throughout His creation. When one looks around all of creation one should be able to see the evidence of God's work. Let me give you a few examples:

- Siblings may look similar, but not exactly alike, except for a few twins. There's variety.

- Some species of birds that fit within the same family have different colors.

- Some birds swim and fly, other cannot fly at all.

- Dogs maybe dogs but aren't you all glad not all are Rottweilers or Bulldogs?

The variety of creation is no accident. Look at the colors, the different animals, the stability of our solar system and the magnificence of us. Whenever one looks around through the eyes of faith one can see what God has made and how magnificent He is. We accept God only through our faith. If one has no faith, one can neither please God nor love Him.

Peter encouraged the Christians who had based their salvation upon the fact, that despite being "distressed by various trials", they remained focused on their future hope in Christ by faith. Now, these people we know were historically under a constant bombardment of suffering and persecution. They were suffering and being persecuted for various reasons, many of which were common for that day, but a few specifics:

- *Suffering because they were living godly lives and doing what was good and right (1 Peter 2:19–23; 3:14–18; 4:1–4, 15–19).*

- *Others were suffering reproach for the name of Christ (1 Peter 4:14) and being railed at by unsaved people (1 Peter 3:9–10).[1]*

Peter described their faith more valuable than gold which results in praise, honor and glory for Jesus. (Verse 7) Here is the grabber, *"and though you have not seen Him, you love Him, and though you do not*

> **You haven't seen Jesus but you love Him.**

see Him now, but believe in Him, you greatly rejoice with joy inexpressible and full of glory." Unlike Peter who had seen and walked with Jesus, these Christians had not seen Jesus, yet they loved Him deeply and believed in Him.

The English language can be very inexact. The word "believe" contains an idea of understanding or head knowledge. We believe in facts we've been taught in school, like the distance from the Earth to our sun is 92 million miles. We believe the Earth is round because we've been told and pictures from NASA show it to be round. But the biblical word believe is not something we accept with our minds, it is faith, an acceptance of truth in which we are willing to commit our lives. Belief in Jesus means we are willing to trust Him with our lives and eternity deeply enough that we're willing to risk our lives or give complete ownership to Him.

Peter's recipients knew Jesus intimately even though they had never seen Him. They knew of God's love for them and were willing to be His children and Peter would be encouraging them to remain faithful and obedient despite hardships.

Jesus said, *"If anyone loves Me, he will keep My word,"* indicates a belief or faith. The belief or faith of genuine Christians is not in a concept or idea, but in the person, Jesus. Jesus demonstrated His submission to God the Father and modeled the power and authority over illness, death and even nature. Jesus was the Son of God and God has raised Him from the dead and He had walked with a large number of people afterward. People for 20 centuries have, by faith, accepted this fact and surrendered their lives and will to Jesus.

Obedience grows out of one's love relationship with the Lord. If one has had an encounter with the Living God, one cannot help but sense and experience His great love. His love is unique to Him. The man-made gods (idols, images, or materialist gods of the American culture) offer nothing for your devotion or attention. Man-made gods cannot love you. They can neither care for you nor provide for you. They merely exist within one's mind. How can one love anything or anyone man-made when the love of God Almighty through Jesus, His Son exists?

> *Obedience to God can only come from one's love for Him.*

Obedience is neither a set of rules to follow nor a relative truth. Obedience is a way of life established through an encounter with Christ. Encountering the person of Jesus is transforming. It is difficult for "proof seekers" to accept this truth because so much of what bombards us promises "life transforming" benefits that make false or temporary claims. Sure, a kitchen gadget might change your life if all you do every waking moment is cook. But can a kitchen gadget or invention comfort you when you are depressed? Can a gadget answer a prayer? Can a gadget give you a joy that surpasses the events of life? No! Only Christ can do these things.

There are many people who try to substitute obedience with works or partial obedience. Today's world gives us many opportunities to self-satisfy this great need, but look at what Jesus said about obedience to Him:

> *"He who believes in the Son has eternal life; but he who does not obey the Son will not see life, but the wrath of God abides on him."* (John 3:36)

> *"On that day, when evening came, He said to them, 'Let us go over to the other side.' Leaving the crowd, they took Him along with them in the boat, just as He was; and other boats*

were with Him. And there arose a fierce gale of wind, and the waves were breaking over the boat so much that the boat was already filling up. Jesus Himself was in the stern, asleep on the cushion; and they woke Him and said to Him, 'Teacher, do You not care that we are perishing?' And He got up and rebuked the wind and said to the sea, 'Hush, be still.' And the wind died down and it became perfectly calm. And He said to them, 'Why are you afraid? How is it that you have no faith?' They became very much afraid and said to one another, 'Who then is this, that even the wind and the sea obey Him?' (Mark 4:35–41)

"'Not everyone who says to Me, 'Lord, Lord,' will enter the kingdom of heaven, but he who does the will of My Father who is in heaven will enter. Many will say to Me on that day, 'Lord, Lord, did we not prophesy in Your name, and in Your name cast out demons, and in Your name perform many miracles?' And then I will declare to them, I never knew you; depart from Me, you who practice lawlessness.'" (Matthew 7:21–26)

Obedience to Christ is a serious matter when one's eternal presence with God is at stake. In addition, one receives a great reward. This reward is the deep love of the Heavenly Father.

Obedience to God grows out of trust in Him. Some people have distrust for everything and everyone. Others easily trust because it is in their nature. The third group has a trust that must be earned over time. I have counseled many divorced couples that are considering remarriage. Sometimes this situation can be a ticking time-bomb and others a piece of cake, depending on their trust issues.

One man discovered his wife of three years had a revolving door of lovers in her life. He tried and tried to trust her again but couldn't and finally divorced. Many individuals have experienced similar situations and went on to live in a happy and harmonious marriage, but the return of trust took a great deal of time and had to be handled like a box of dynamite – very carefully.

Trusting God, for most people, comes from a growing relationship. As one walks with God, one hears God speaking through the Holy Spirit. He gives comfort in our times of trouble. He gives us strength when we are weak. Our relationship with Him yields a heavenly joy because our sin-sick soul has been healed. As we yield to His leadership, we experience Him. Each encounter with the Living God can build our spiritual lives and trust in Him. Trusting God with the smaller and simple issues can give us an assurance that He truly cares and lives in us. As these encounters grow, one's trust can grow into a beautiful and large trust.

Trusting and loving God is the center of obedience. Some people can follow a set of rules, that too is obedience. This is much like obeying speed limit signs. There's one tremendous difference. Speed limit signs are not a person, just a metal sign on a metal pole. God is a person, not like any other, but never-the-less a person, who wants us to freely love Him and follow His wishes for our life.

Each of us in our intimacy with God want to obey Him. It may be a struggle at first, but over time gets easier and easier. Everyone can begin the journey of obedience, just pick a beginning point and go from there. I suggest the first place one needs to begin is in believer's baptism. This is considered the first step of obedience. Churches have different ideas about teaching the Christian disciple-making process but seek one that has a vibrant disciple-making ministry that can teach you doctrine, praying, living, witnessing and ministering. There is no gold in the U.S. Treasury that is as valuable as this part of your obedience. Don't hurry through it. Savor this time like it was your favorite momma-cooked dish or sitting beside a gently rushing stream under a shade tree relaxing.

3 - "If anyone loves Me, he will keep My word; and My Father will love him,"

You heard me say earlier that God loves everyone. What might be different about this love? God cares for and wants the best for every human being, but He does not walk or live in everyone He loves, only those who are obedient.

There is a love or concern for all of humankind but then there is a special "covenant love" for God's children. Each child of God lives in the New Covenant of Christ. This is a mutual or two-sided love. The love in John 3:16 is a one-sided love from God.

The truth of this passage applies to an individual, but also corporate church. People can neither experience the love or blessings from another's relationship with the Lord, but in the body of Christ, we all form one body as if we were one individual. Each person reaps the benefit of their own personal relationship with Christ and the church as a whole either experiences the blessings of Jesus from the corporate life or not.

Have you ever asked, "Why are churches dying? Why are people not interested in the spiritual life? Many churches are discovering their corporate obedience to Jesus is responsible for growth. Take for example the XYZ Church at Jerusalem in Acts. This church had a corporate or whole congregational experience with Jesus on the Day of Pentecost.

Let me begin answering the question, "Why are churches dying" by relating a story from the book of Acts. Jesus told His followers gave them some final instructions just before His ascension in Acts 1:4–5:

> *"Gathering them together, He commanded them not to leave Jerusalem, but to wait for what the Father had promised, "Which," He said, 'you heard of from Me; for John baptized*

with water, but you will be baptized with the Holy Spirit not many days from now'"

His followers returned to the upper room in Jerusalem where they had gathered for the Last Supper. (verse 1:13) There were gathered about 120 people including Mary, the mother of Jesus, Jesus' brothers, His disciples and several women. There they devoted themselves to prayer. (verse 1:14). On the day of Pentecost, the group gathered, and the Scriptures describe them as still "all together". (Verse 2:1) Then, suddenly, the promise of Jesus in verse 1:4 was fulfilled when the Holy Spirit came upon the group described as, *"And suddenly there came from heaven a noise like a violent rushing wind, and it filled the whole house where they were sitting. And there appeared to them tongues as of fire distributing themselves, and they rested on each one of them. And they were all filled with the Holy Spirit and began to speak with other tongues, as the Spirit was giving them utterance."* (Acts 2:2–4) The Holy Spirit filled them all with His presence and they were of one heart, one mind and one mission. This event was a corporate (entire body of Christ) occurrence.

Peter preached a powerful sermon (Acts 2:14-40). The Lord Jesus was preached for the forgiveness of sins and immediately a spontaneous invitation resulted in about 3,000 souls saved. (2:42) That, my folks, was the beginning of the church. As a group, souls were saved, lives were changed, and the power of Jesus was upon the people.

This new church was excited because the corporate body had experienced the Risen Savior that day during Pentecost. They were empowered and ready to be the "salt and light" of the world. The writer of Acts, Dr. Luke recorded this:

"They were continually devoting themselves to the apostles' teaching and to fellowship, to the breaking of bread and to

> *prayer. Everyone kept feeling a sense of awe; and many wonders and signs were taking place through the apostles. And all those who had believed were together and had all things in common; and they began selling their property and possessions and were sharing them with all, as anyone might have need. Day by day continuing with one mind in the temple, and breaking bread from house to house, they were taking their meals together with gladness and sincerity of heart, praising God and having favor with all the people. And the Lord was adding to their number day by day those who were being saved."* (Acts 2:42–47)

The Light of Christ had a transforming effect upon a whole group of people, not just a few select. The newly formed body of Christ not only had stood on shaking ground at Pentecost, but now had their entire lives shaken to the core and were filled with the presence of the Risen Savior, Jesus. Their hearts and minds had changed and as a result, their priorities had changed. They had an understanding that this world they lived in was temporary and so the material possessions they had meant nothing.

> *"And the congregation of those who believed were of one heart and soul; and not one of them claimed that anything belonging to him was his own, but all things were common property to them. And with great power the apostles were giving testimony to the resurrection of the Lord Jesus, and abundant grace was upon them all. For there was not a needy person among them, for all who were owners of land or houses would sell them and bring the proceeds of the sales and lay them at the apostles' feet, and they would be distributed to each as any had need."* (4:32-35)

The entire congregational life was changed. They were not concerned with great and marvelous buildings or suits and ties; each individual was deeply moved by the Spirit of the Living God to continue the ministry of Jesus. They had a deep concern, not only for their own church family, but for their community as well.

The Light of Christ transformed the church and He built a witness of ordinary people, who loved Him deeply and were obedient to His command to "not to leave Jerusalem, but to wait for what the Father had promised, 'Which,' He said, "you heard of from Me; for John baptized with water, but you will be baptized with the Holy Spirit not many days from now." They had experienced the love of the Father (John 14:23) and God had made His home in and with them.

> *The presence of the Light of Jesus will transform the whole church*

Faithfulness is the issue in receiving the promised love and presence of God. Jesus taught a parable about faithfulness that applies to every believer of Christ and all churches. In the Parable of the Talents Jesus gave a story with a lesson, as in all parables which apply to our faithfulness whether as individuals or the church as a whole.

> *"'For it is just like a man about to go on a journey, who called his own <u>slaves and entrusted</u> his possessions to them. To one he gave five talents, to another, two, and to another, one, each according to his own ability; and he went on his journey. Immediately the one who had received the five talents went and traded with them and gained five more talents. In the same manner the one who had received the two talents gained two more. But he who received the one talent went away, and dug a hole in the ground and hid his master's money. Now after a long time the master of those slaves came and settled accounts with them. The one who had received the five talents came up and brought five more talents, saying, 'Master, you entrusted five talents to me. See, I have gained five more talents.' His master said to him, 'Well done, good and faithful slave. You*

were faithful with a few things, I will put you in charge of many things; enter into the joy of your master.' Also, the one who had received the two talents came up and said, 'Master, you entrusted two talents to me. See, I have gained two more talents.' His master said to him, 'Well done, good and faithful slave. You were faithful with a few things, I will put you in charge of many things; enter into the joy of your master.' And the one also who had received the one talent came up and said, 'Master, I knew you to be a hard man, reaping where you did not sow and gathering where you scattered no seed. 'And I was afraid, and went away and hid your talent in the ground. See, you have what is yours.' But his master answered and said to him, 'You wicked, lazy slave, you knew that I reap where I did not sow and gather where I scattered no seed. 'Then you ought to have put my money in the bank, and on my arrival I would have received my money back with interest. 'Therefore, take away the talent from him and give it to the one who has the ten talents.' "For to everyone who has, more shall be given, and he will have an abundance; but from the one who does not have, even what he does have shall be taken away. 'Throw out the worthless slave into the outer darkness; in that place there will be weeping and gnashing of teeth.'"
(Matthew 25:14–30)

I pray you see the parallel between this parable and our lives as individuals and the corporate church. Here are some highlights

- *Jesus is the Master. He left behind his servants (you and I) to continue to accomplish His mission. (25:14)*

- *He gives us different assignments according to our spiritual gifts.(25:15)*

- *Each person has different results but the same ministry. (25:16-18)*

> • *The Master returns (Jesus' second coming) and holds us responsible for what we have done with our assignment (love your neighbor, Great Commission and etc.)(25:19-30)*

If you will notice Jesus' approved of the first two servants' efforts because they actively sought to fulfill their Master's wish. The Master said, "Well done, good and faithful slave. You were faithful with a few things, I will put you in charge of many things; enter into the joy of your master." (25:21) The second man did not have the same results but remember each were given according to their abilities. Jesus told the second man the same as the first, "Well done, good and faithful slave. You were faithful with a few things, I will put you in charge of many things; enter into the joy of your master."

But the third man, Jesus condemned. (25:26-28)

> *"'But his master answered and said to him, 'You wicked, lazy slave, you knew that I Reap where I did not sow and gather where I scattered no seed. Then you ought to have put my money in the bank, and on my arrival I would have received my money back with interest. Therefore take away the talent from him, and give it to the one who has the ten talents.'"*

You may say, "I've never heard this story or its application before!" Don't you truly believe we have a great need in our day and time to know the Truth of the Gospel? Is our world suffering? Have we truly been the salt and light of the world? Some have, and many are struggling with their Christ-given mission.

We can gather a great truth from Jesus in verse 29, "For to everyone who has, more shall be given, and he will have an abundance; but from the one who does not have, even what he does have shall be taken away." Have you ever wondered why some churches are growing and others are slowly dying or already dead? I have found throughout the nation the same root cause, "they have either forgotten their mission or failed to fulfill it!"

> *People and churches find increasing abundance of God's provisions when both are faithful to the Word of God*

Please let me explain. We've been given an outward command, "Go and make disciples" (Matthew 28:18-20). We are commanded to, "Proclaim the Good News". Yet in many churches people sit and listen but believe if anyone is supposed to do this it is the pastor and staff. Wrong! The responsibility is given to every born-again believer. But only those who are obedient get to hear Jesus' message, "Well done, good and faithful slave. You were faithful with a few things, I will put you in charge of many things; enter into the joy of your master.'

The Lord Jesus Christ blesses those churches who are obedient in their love, not just inwardly, but outwardly too. We come into the house of God to worship Him and leave to do ministry. If we are unfaithful as a church, why would He want to send more people to learn disobedience and give us a false hope that we are being obedient? He sends people to church who are faithful in worship, ministry, evangelism, discipleship and fellowship. Jesus sends people to a praying church. He sends them to a church that has an intentional and purpose-filled disciple-making process. He sends people to churches that are willing to love the "unlovable" – you know, those unlike "us". The Lord God leads people to churches who are more interested in the physical, emotional and spiritual needs of others rather than budgets and buildings.

Churches experiencing a decline do so for a reason, it is their faithfulness and obedience issue. Many churches have become social clubs that say, "Us and no more". These churches are similar to the third servant of the Parable of the Talents, unfaithful.

What a joy it is to do the Master's will! There have been occasions in worship that I get so excited about the moving of the Holy Spirit that I have almost forgotten to take up the offering. When I have presented a witness and people have responded, I leap with joy, inwardly and feel the Lord saying, "Well done good and faithful servant."

As I have spoken with people in different churches and their leadership, I have asked this question, "What is it you single-most spiritual struggle in your life and the life of your church? They usually respond, "Being obedient to Christ in loving others (ministry outside the walls) and evangelism." I have come to anticipate that response, but I pray for them and encourage them to begin being faithful to all Jesus has commanded.

There have been many people to come to me and ask, "Our church as a whole seems to be uncaring for the needs of people and the lost condition of folks, what am I supposed to do?" My encouragement to them has been this, "I would encourage you, as an individual follower of Jesus to be faithful and obedient to Him, whether anyone else is or not."

But to the leadership of the church, I challenge you to be faithful men of God and lead your church in complete obedience, according to God's Holy Word, not by a few people who seem to have no heart for true, biblical, Spirit-led ministry. The church, should, also be walking in the Light of Jesus. There is a great cost in being a faithful leader of His church, can you pay that price?

The Light shines upon and illuminates the truths of God, huh? If the leadership is walking in the light, the Holy Spirit will testify to the truths Jesus taught and guide you into the ministry of His church, as Jesus told Peter, "feed my sheep". (John 12:17)

The Holy Spirit reveals and reminds us of all that Jesus taught. If we're listening, we don't have to have a great memory to remember it all, we only have to have a sensitive Spirit to the voice of God. He will remind us. Sometimes He will remind us over and over. Aren't you thankful that God doesn't give us only one slim chance of hearing His mighty voice and responding? I am. Sometimes I have had to hear the same voice more than once. But you can bet your last dollar, I respond as quickly as I can.

When we experience the love of God, we are moved to obey Him. When we obey Him, He comes and makes His home in our lives. Then, we have the ever-lasting presence of God Almighty in us.

9 GOD COMES TO LIVE IN US

"and We will come to him and make Our home with him"

Jehovah God gave the prophet Isaiah a prophecy in the 7th Century B.C. about the Messiah. He told Isaiah, *"Therefore the Lord Himself will give you a sign: Behold, a virgin will be with child and bear a son, and she will call His name Immanuel"*. (Isaiah 7:14) And behold, one can see in the New Testament, nearly 700 years later this revelation to Isaiah coming true.

> *"Behold, the virgin shall be with child and shall bear a Son, and they shall call His name Immanuel," which translated means, "God with us." (Matthew 1:23)*

Do you remember what God did in the Garden of Eden with Adam and Eve? Moses recorded in Genesis 3:8 where God walked in the coolness of the Garden where they lived. After sin entered through this couple, God no longer walked among men, generally speaking. In Leviticus 26:12 God promised to walk among His people. The overwhelming evidence for this verb is "go with" or "be among".

The revelation to Joseph, Mary's husband was much more than "being with us" or "going with us," God was actually here in the person of Jesus and that's why the angel told Joseph, "the virgin will be with child and shall bear a Son, and they shall call His name "Immanuel, which translates means, "God with Us." God was with us in the presence of His Son, Jesus. He walked among the people for slightly over 3 years until His crucifixion, death, burial, resurrection and ascension.

Jesus prepared His disciples for His soon-to-be departure. Jesus' public ministry was about to come to an end because of the events of the Passion Week: death, burial, and resurrection. It appears as if the disciples had the idea He was leaving them behind, forever. John 14:1–4 sets the stage for this:

> *"'Do not let your heart be troubled; believe in God, believe also in Me. In My Father's house are many dwelling places;*

> *if it were not so, I would have told you; for I go to prepare a place for you. If I go and prepare a place for you, I will come again and receive you to Myself, that where I am, there you may be also. And you know the way where I am going'"*

Through much of the history of Israel knew God dwelled in the Holy of Holies within the temple. There they offered sin sacrifices and gift sacrifices. God was hidden behind a huge veil between the Holy Place and the Holy of Holies. This veil (curtain) was sixty feet long and draped from the top to the floor. This was the veil or curtain torn from top to bottom at Jesus' death.

God had promised through Moses that He would choose a particular location as the dwelling place for His name. (Deuteronomy 12:11) Only in this location was Israel allowed to sacrifice to Him. (Deuteronomy 12:13-14) The temple is where males of Israel would come three times per year to celebrate major festivals of faith that God has established in His Law. The temple was a permanent site replacing the temporary tabernacles while Israel was in their wilderness years.

The Temple was completed in the fourth year of King Solomon's reign, approximately 960 B.C. When King Solomon dedicated the Temple to the Lord, a visible appearance of the "glory of the Lord" descended from heaven and filled the temple. (2 Chronicles 7:1-3) This is the event marking the coming of the presence of the Lord to the Temple.

The Temple complex was modified several times throughout the centuries. The original Temple was destroyed by the invading Babylonians in the 7th Century B.C. and rebuilt by the returning Jews after they returned from captivity. King Herod the Great greatly expanded the Temple in the year of 20 B.C. This was the Temple spoke of in the New Testament during Jesus' ministry.

The temple was comprised of several different locations within the complex and each had their own importance and function. At the center of the temple complex was the "Holy of Holies". This is where the presence of the Lord resided. The "Holy of Holies" contained the Arc of the Covenant which itself contained the Ten

Commandments on stone tablets. This portion of the Temple complex was secluded from the other portions. Only the Chief Priest was allowed into the Holy of Holies on the Day of Atonement with the sacrifice for sin.

Until Jesus' death on the cross no one entered the Holy of Holies because it was separated by a huge curtain measuring 60 feet in length and some estimates indicate it was several inches thick. The moment of Jesus' death, the temple veil was torn from top to bottom. (Matthew 27:51) When one is reading the story in the Gospels, it is easy to miss the importance. The veil was extremely heavy-duty wall of material many inches thick.

The tearing of the temple veil was to signify God tore it not man, as evidenced from top to bottom. It signified that God was making Himself available to all mankind, not just the Jews. This supernatural event took place at the very moment Jesus drew His last breath and said, "It is over!" Jesus' body had been crucified and the Temple veil ripped, signifying God had come through Jesus to dwell among His people, as evidenced in Acts 2, the Day of Pentecost. Jesus was indeed fulfilling His promise to His disciples (John 14:1-4) when He said, "I go and prepare a place for you."

> *God tore the temple veil to bring Himself to us*
>
> ***How much love is that?***

God gave us an eternal promise to be with His children in Deuteronomy 31:6. He told Moses to tell the people, *"Be strong and courageous, do not be afraid or tremble at them, for the LORD your God is the one who goes with you. He will not fail you or forsake you."*

Jesus repeated God's eternal promise when He said, "I am with you always, even to the end of the age." (Matthew 28:20) The "you" in this passage known as the Great Commission applies to all who follow Jesus. In the meantime, we celebrate the presence of God with us (Immanuel) by the presence of the Holy Spirit. Jesus is a part of every genuine believer's life. He dwells in the believer. He speaks to the believer. He directs the believer's lives.

Unfortunately, too many times we believe Jesus leads us in jobs to accept or what school to attend. He does, but He's interested in so much more that we leave out. He directs us in our life with Him, our worship, our prayers, our ministry and our discipleship needs. He wants to direct your whole life.

If you have ever purchased something, a home or a car, you may have had to put down a deposit. In the business world this is called a "good faith deposit". The deposit is a sign of your serious intent to purchase or forfeit the deposited money.

The Apostle Paul understood the fact that Jesus would return some day to bring together all of those who had placed their faith in Him and awaited eternity with Him in heaven. Jesus was serious and left us a deposit, the Holy Spirit. The Holy Spirit is our "good faith deposit" that Jesus would indeed return to claim us to Himself. We see this truth in Ephesians 1:13-14, below.

> *"In Him, you also, after listening to the message of truth, the gospel of your salvation—having also believed, you were sealed in Him with the Holy Spirit of promise, who is given as a pledge of our inheritance, with a view to the redemption of God's own possession, to the praise of His glory."* (Ephesians 1:13–14)

The Holy Spirit is the pledge of our inheritance with a view to the redemption of God's own possession. One day the Christian will inherit his/her eternal life and it will be to the praise of God's glory. Until that time occurs those who follow Jesus in an obedient relationship have His presence with them.

Jesus shows you and I the way by the His Light

Jesus showing the way by His light is more than a walk down a dark path; the light is our guidance in life and ministry. As His representatives or ambassadors (2 Corinthians 5:20) a Christians' function is to continue the ministry of Jesus while we are on earth and He is preparing for us our eternal presence in Heaven.

If you have ever been a leader in any organization or endeavor, you know you must have a vision or goal. As a leader you must lead by example and an inspiration those who follow you. A leader must have a plan in order to succeed.

Church leadership needs the qualities of a visionary or God-inspired goal setter who leads by example and is an inspiration to those who follow him, his flock. In the first two decades of the 21st Century we see undeniable proof that many of our churches are slowly dying. Attendance continues to decline because of four possible and unfortunate truths:

1. Many have taken their eyes off the Lord Jesus.

2. There are many folks in leadership merely continuing to do what they have known to do before.

3. Perhaps they are ministering in their own strength and abilities rather than the power of the Lord God.

4. Or perhaps they are not walking in the truth of God's Light and presence

If an individual is walking in the Light, then he or she is under the inspiration and guidance of God's Holy Spirit, as was Jesus, Himself. When an obstacle in life and ministry is encountered, one should pause and await further instructions from the Lord and not give up. Then and only then proceed.

When the Bride of Christ, the church, is walking in the Light the entire body has several powerful and victorious outcomes.

1. They hear the voice of God speaking and know precisely what to do and how to do it.

2. The whole assembly of believers become of one heart and mind, as in Acts.

3. They experience the power of the Lord Jesus, His encouragement and courage.

4. There is a great joy and excitement flowing through the church family because they are experiencing God, Himself.

5. Their church is growing numerically by evangelism and spiritually through discipleship.

6. There is an unexplainable power of the Light which draws humanity to the person of Jesus.

If a church lacks the power and victory of Christ and they are slowly dying. The local church's demise isn't the community's fault, but they are the real sufferers. Following World War II when soldiers were returning from war, they were building or buying homes in the suburbs. This was a new-found time of prosperity when families that had come from farms during the Great Depression to a time in which they had money in their pockets, burning to be spent.

During this time a popular phrase was developed, especially among churches, "If you build it they will come." That was once true, but no longer. I have heard more than once this said by people inside the churches I pastored, "Pastor, people know where the church is. If they want to come, they will." My first response was, "Well you don't know people. You also don't know the Lord, Jesus!"

> *Christians are the "called out ones"; called out into our communities to share the love of God through **Jesus***

Let me see if I can drive my point home. Have you ever seen a television commercial? Do you suppose a commercial is meant to entertain you? I use them as time get popcorn or more coffee. Commercials are to entice you to buy their product. The commercial writers use women in slinky dresses and men in tuxedos to impress you with the elegance of using their product or to show you how tiring using a fork to feed yourself can be and you need "Robo Stuffer" the effortless way to eat 55 gallons of spaghetti.

A large portion of our society today does not know what that building (church) down the street is there to do. They haven't been in worship or Bible study. They do not know about the Word of God or His righteousness. How are they to know about redemption in Christ unless we go and tell them? Jesus commands we go and tell. (Matthew 28:18-20) There is no plan B.

The church are the ones called out into the community to minister and present their witness and the Good News that Jesus came to seek and save those who are lost. There are signs on many exit doors of churches that have this phrase, "Through these doors is your mission field." This is not a catchy phrase, but a biblical truth. To be otherwise is not walking in the Light!

Many churches have depended heavily upon programs and functions that drain the time and finances away from the redeemed so that they do not have time left to go out into the community, build relationships and present the Gospel. Christians' main function is not eating. Outreach is not inviting someone to lunch at the church, although that can be helpful. People have a great need to humble themselves before the Lord and ask Him, "What do You, O Lord, want in my life? Is there something missing? Am I walking in obedience? Am I effective for Your Kingdom? Await His answer and be ready for what He says, then do it.

The local church should be like a rudder steering a ship or plane, steering a community toward the port of righteousness. Should a person or church not be walking the light of Jesus and are purely drifting through time, then that is the evidence of the lack of the Power of Almighty God present in and through the Holy Spirit. Without the Light guiding the church's path, the church is just an address on Google Maps.

Would you agree anything healthy is growing? Healthy economies grow and prosper. A healthy yard grows lush, green grass. A healthy puppy grows into maturity. A healthy baby grows into an adult. Healthy churches grow too. The Body of Christ has to grow by first experiencing the Person of Jesus Christ. I have discovered we have to "be" before we can "do". Christians must be the people of God before we can do the work of God. Sometimes I have found the opposite, we want to "do" to "be". That does not follow the Light's plan. The Disciples and the Apostle Paul are great examples of this truth. All who proclaim the might Word of God must spend time in His presence and be taught how to correctly divide the Word. Every person in the pew is expected to do the same by Our Savior.

We are to teach all that Jesus taught. Discipleship is one of the essentials to experiencing Christ. Obedience to the Word of God is another essential to experiencing Christ. Despite many Pastors' sermons many people's lives are not exposed to deep, thorough discipleship. Sermons are aimed at teaching, but more especially worship inviting a response of acceptance of that day's Word and implementation. Discipleship is, according to Jesus' model that which teaches deep theology and ministry to the community.

Several church leaders are addressing the problem of the diminishing size of many local churches. We are living in the post-church age, but I believe there is more truth to the situation than "the times we live within". First there is a multitude of church leaders that do not want help. There seems to be an apathy or lack of compassion for the lost and dying world, unless it sits in their pew. There is help for struggling churches but offers go without response. We may watch a home-improvement show or cooking show, but why aren't we as troubled about a hurting, lost world? Might it be due to a lack of walking in the Light?

I personally need the light of Christ every moment of my life. Someone commented recently that I have an appreciation for God's Word. My response was, "Appreciation, no, love and dependence upon, yes." The voice of God has become more important to me than anyone else's voice or opinion. How often do we reverse this priority?

Walking in the light of Christ is crucial. It is like insulin to a diabetic. It's like anti-rejection medications to a transplant recipient. It is like food, water and sleep to everyone. Many live because of these provisions. God has made an even greater provision, His Son, Jesus, the Light of the World. One cannot live successfully in this life without Him. One will not live in Heaven if one does not walk in His Light!

> *To a Christian Walking in the Light is as crucial as insulin to a diabetic or cardiac medicine to a heart patient*

Every person on earth needs the Light of Christ to show them the way to God's righteousness. When the Light shows the way, one has a choice of following the illuminated path Jesus has shown us or ignoring it. The Lord will never force a person to make a decision to surrender their lives to Him. This is something that we each must decide to do. This decision is not a family decision, it is a personal decision.

The decision to walk in the Light, as Jesus is in the light sometimes is not easily made, although it should be. One must accept the truths of God's Word by faith. Faith is not by sight or necessarily a tangible proof, but the acceptance of Who God says He is as revealed in His Holy Word. Trying to prove God is like emptying the oceans of all the water with a teaspoon.

By faith people are saved (Ephesians 2:8-9) not by our works. Some people have relied upon a relative's faith, but that won't work. Other have said, "Look at what I have done for God!" That's works and it won't work, either.

One might also say, "Well I believe in Jesus." The word believe in the American society does not mean what it did in the Bible. The Apostle James said, "You believe that God is one. You do well; the demons also believe, and shudder. (James 2:19) Believing in Jesus means you are convinced He is the Messiah, the Son of God, the Lord, and God Himself. You accept His Word, authority and power. You recognize He alone is the only way to salvation and to God.

One whom believes in Jesus empties oneself of all human will in favor of God's will. This person is willing to sell one's self into the bondage of the Lord God and be His servant. A believer is willing to submit one's self for a disciple-making process that should insure a healthy spiritual life in Christ.

In obedience, one needs to become a part of a church family that believes and practices all that Jesus came to earth and did, followed by believer's baptism.

10 HOW TO LIGHT THE PATH OF GOD'S PRESENCE IN YOU

Jesus answered and said to him, "Truly, truly, I say to you, unless one is born again he cannot see the kingdom of God." (John 3:3)

Several years ago, a friend told a story that I will never forget. John had recently gone to pastor a new church. He spoke to the Deacons about visiting the community and sharing Christ with the neighborhood. One of the Deacons spoke up and said, "Pastor, I have lived here all my life. Everyone in the community has been saved.

After a few minutes of discussion, the Deacon that voiced his opinion agreed to go calling on homes within the neighborhood. John, the Pastor bet a steak dinner they would find at least one and probably more that had never made a profession of faith. Both men agreed to buy the other one a steak dinner if he was wrong.

One of the first few houses the Pastor and Deacon visited they found a man at home. This man truly had been known by the Deacon for many years. John said the visit was cordial and he asked the man, "Have you ever made a profession of faith in Jesus and asked Him to save you?" How do you think the man responded? If you thought the man said, "Yes, I have" then you didn't win the all expense trip to the salad bar.

The man of the house said, "No, Pastor, I haven't." John wasn't surprised, but the Deacon surely was. The Deacon's deep belief that everyone around him was saved got shot full of holes. Well, that day one man prayed to receive Jesus as his Lord and Savior and John got a steak dinner.

The reason why I told this story is this: too many times we believe moral behavior indicates an eternal decision to follow Jesus. There is nothing further from the truth. For many decades, if not several centuries, Americans have been raised to be moral people. We are taught we should not steal, kill, cuss, lie, rape, pillage or chew tobacco. We have been taught a more gentile way of life that centers of one's behavior in society. But, there is a far distance between moral behavior and walking in the Light of Christ.

Moral behavior is called a societal norm. A norm is an expected behavior defined by Merriam-Webster Dictionary as, "a principle of right action binding upon the members of a group and serving to guide, control, or regulate proper and acceptable behavior." In other words, it is a behavior society accepts as acceptable behavior. Moral behavior, at least to me, might be considered similarly to manners. If you live in the West, one doesn't go into a house wearing the same boots one wore while working the cattle.

For some, following Christ is a societal norm rather than a life transforming experience of the Living God. "Going to church" is what one does! Avoid four letter words (like four?) is not what a Christian does. America has been a cultural Christian society. Nearly everyone believes themselves to be Christian. The top reasons are:

1. One or more of their parents went to church, at least occasionally.
2. They went to Sunday School when they were young kids but haven't really had the time now.
3. They have been in church since before they were born.
4. A class of children or youth they were in had several that "decided" to become a Christian.
5. They made a "profession of faith" because they were scared they would die and go to hell.

6. Their grand momma or momma told them they had to become a Christian.
7. The preacher scared the stuffins' out of them one Sunday.
8. They did something that they thought would get them into serious trouble and they wanted Jesus on their side.
9. They want to be in heaven just in case God and Jesus is real.
10. They want to date or marry a really sweet, good-looking girl who is a Christian or their wife nags them saying, "I don't want the kids to be alone in heaven without their daddy.
11. Their parents had them baptized when they were a few days old.
12. They are moral people they have never: stolen, raped or pillaged
13. Someone told me I was a good person.
14. They were born sinless
15. I don't believe God sends anyone to hell
16. They give money to church and charities

Personally, I did not fit into the "Top Ten." Number 16 applied to me. Yep, you are right there is no number 16 on the list. Here's my testimony:

A Godly lady I worked with invited me to Bible study (Sunday School). I like the people and felt good about going. After Bible study I would go to morning worship. I cannot remember much except I was doing the "norm".

The church was holding a revival and I went. I can't say I felt a compulsion, I went. While there the speaker spoke about dying and going to hell or something like that. The exact message is quite blurry, but I do vividly remember what happened.

I do remember feeling a truly uncomfortable feeling. It was a feeling

I had never experienced, but it was certainly horrible and painful. I began to feel the weight of my sin on my own shoulders and an extreme guilt for my sin. I remember holding on to the back of the pew as if I were on a roller coaster. Then came the moment I surrendered my life to Christ, asked Him to forgive me of my sins and become the Lord of my life.

That night I gave my life to Jesus and it has never been the same again. There have been moments I have strayed. I will never say I've lived a perfect life for Him, but I certainly strive to do that now.

Jesus has been there every moment of my life since. Let me give you an illustration from driving a car. On a journey it is prudent to look where you're going. In my own spiritual life, I cannot see where I am going, but I can see where I have been. Personally, I call this looking at life through the rear-view mirror. I can see where the Father has saved my physical life on many occasions. I can see where I was weak, and He gave me strength. I can look at the temptations in my life and see where He has moved me to remain faithful.

To walk in the Light of God's presence in you, you will need to read the Gospels. Be willing to read slowly and allow the Holy Spirit to speak to you. I would advise you to pay special attention to the teachings of Jesus and see how your life matches up to the Word of God rather than relying upon your own opinion.

Let me give you a few to think about:

Do you have someone you need to forgive for something?

> *"For if you forgive others for their transgressions, your heavenly Father will also forgive you. But if you do not forgive others, then your Father will not forgive your transgressions."* (Matthew 6:14–15).

Forgiveness is given to you for your sins as you forgive others of their wrongs done to do.

Do you worry?

> *"Do not worry then, saying, 'What will we eat? or 'What will we drink?' or 'What will we wear for clothing?' For the Gentiles eagerly seek all these things; for your Heavenly Father knows that you need all these things. But seek first His kingdom and His righteousness, and all these things will be added to you. So do not worry about tomorrow; for tomorrow will care for itself. Each day has enough trouble of its own.* (Matthew 6:31–34)

Worry shows a God problem. The problem is you do not trust Him to provide for you or you have spent your life providing for yourself and when you are no longer able to do this, you fear. Do you judge others?

> *"Do not judge so that you will not be judged. For in the way you judge, you will be judged; and by your standard of measure, it will be measured to you. Why do you look at the speck that is in your brother's eye, but do not notice the log that is in your own eye? Or how can you say to your brother, 'Let me take the speck out of your eye,' and behold, the log is in your own eye? You hypocrite, first take the log out of your own eye, and then you will see clearly to take the speck out of your brother's eye.* (Matthew 7:1–5)

Judging means to look unfavorably on the character and actions of others, which leads invariably to the pronouncing of rash, unjust, and unlovely judgments upon them. Jesus pointed to the truth that many try to misinterpret how someone else is doing without taking looking in their own mirror.

> *Are you a compassionate person, caring for the needs of others even if you do not know them?*

Are you truly a compassionate person looking at the needs of others. (Matthew 25:31-46) In our day of individual isolation, we tend not to be concerned with the struggles of other people because we think we have enough to be concern about. This passage is powerful about how we minister to others, whether in our church or not.

Another passage with a parallel truth is the Parable of the Good Samaritan. (Luke 10:30-36) This passage teaches us believers we should be concerned with the welfare and needs of those we don't know. Do you?

There are too many Parables and teachings within the Gospels by Jesus to go into each one. The main thought is to walk in the Light as Jesus is in the light means we obey all of Jesus' teachings. You will find some will cause you great concern, others will challenge you, but the truth still applies after 20 centuries. You may be tempted to say, "This doesn't apply to me." Should you pick and choose which Scriptures apply to you and which do not, I would suggest giving your Bible to someone who does want to learn from God's Word.

Let me remind you of what Jesus said in John 14:6, *"I am the way, and the truth, and the life; no one comes to the Father but through Me."* The only way to eternal life with God is through His Son, Jesus. He also instructs us "He who has My commandments and keeps them is the one who loves Me; and he who loves Me will be loved by My Father, and I will love him and will disclose Myself to him." (John 14:21) God set the standard and Jesus fulfilled it and was Himself obedient to the Father. Do we have any right to tell Almighty God what we will do and what we won't do? God has already answered that question to the Prophet Jeremiah.

- Romans 3:10 - *As it is written: "There is no one righteous, not even one;* (No one is good enough)

- Romans 3:23 - *for all have sinned and fall short of the glory of God,* (Everyone has sinned, we've all made mistakes)

- Romans 5:8 - *But God demonstrates his own love for us in this: While we were still sinners, Christ died for us.* (Because of love, Jesus paid the death penalty for our sins)

- Romans 6:23 - *For the wages of sin is death, but the gift of God is eternal life in Christ Jesus our Lord.* (Eternal life is a free gift from God)

- Romans 10:9 - *That if you confess with your mouth, "Jesus is Lord," and believe in your heart that God raised him from the dead, you will be saved.* (Confess with your mouth and believe in your heart)

- Romans 10:13 – *"for, 'Everyone who calls on the name of the Lord will be saved.'"* (Ask God to save you and He will)

You could pray a similar prayer

I understand that I have sinned. Because of my sin, I deserve death, but You, God, showed Your love for me through Jesus' death. I confess with my mouth and believe in my heart that you raise Jesus from the dead and I want to experience You as my Lord, my God, and my Savior. Please save me and accept my life as I give it to You. Amen!

Next step

If you feel led by the Spirit, give me an email at:

bill@billjerniganministris.org and bear witness about the wonderful decision you have made. I will pray for you and help in any way I can. Immediately find a church you sense the Lord leading you toward and tell the pastor or a counselor during the invitation about the decision you made at home, work or play. Submit yourself for believers' baptism and to be disciple.

May the Lord God of creation and salvation fill you with His presence. More especially, may you walk in The Light of Jesus.

Your servant,

Bill Jernigan

> *"The word which came to Jeremiah from the LORD saying, 'Arise and go down to the potter's house, and there I will announce My words to you.' Then I went down to the potter's house, and there he was, making something on the wheel. But the vessel that he was making of clay was spoiled in the hand of the potter; so he remade it into another vessel, as it pleased the potter to make. Then the word of the LORD came to me saying, 'Can I not, O house of Israel, deal with you as this potter does?' declares the LORD. 'Behold, like the clay in the potter's hand, so are you in My hand, O house of Israel.'"* (Jeremiah 18:1–6)

A follower of Jesus is the disciple (student) and Jesus is the Master. This brings another question. Does the student have the ability to discern which is appropriate and correct or have the right to dictate to the Master that which he or she will or will not do?

> *"A disciple is not above his teacher, nor a slave above his master.* (Matthew 10:24)

Earlier I included a passage from Matthew 25:14-30 about the Parable of the Talents, which I will not repeat again. However, the truth is still the same. The Master has the right to tell His servants what He wants them to do. We are the servants of the Master, Lord God Almighty. I can't really say, "I won't do that Lord," but there have been times I have asked, "How?"

Should we (me included) should ever find that I am not doing what I know to do, disobedience is the order of the day. Walking in the Light means I see what you want, Lord and I will do it. There's an old military saying that's appropriate,

Mine is to not to reason why, my job is to do or die." (Author unknown)

Here is the biblical pattern of understanding leading to salvation

11 TAKING GOD'S LIGHT INTO OUR COMMUNITY

"You are the light of the world. A city set on a hill cannot be hidden; nor does anyone light a lamp and put it under a basket, but on the lampstand, and it gives light to all who are in the house. "Let your light shine before men in such a way that they may see your good works, and glorify your Father who is in heaven. (Matthew 5:14–16)

When you dwell in the light of Jesus by your obedience and He and the Father come and live in you and with you, they want to live through you. They do this through a total-life make-over.

You may have seen programs on television where a person's wardrobe, haircut and makeup are completely redone to improve their highlights and make them more attractive. There have been programs where teams will go into a home and totally make it over again. This is the same application for an individual, too. There's one gigantic exception, God is not remaking the way you look on the inside, He's remaking the way you look on the inside.

The biblical term is called transformation. You may remember from chapter 1 where Jesus' appearance was suddenly and drastically changed. His disciples noticed Jesus and His clothes glowed. Also, you may remember the example I used of a worm entering a cocoon and exiting a butterfly. The worm was transformed or went through a metamorphosis.

It is natural for you and me to struggle with our old way of life contradicting our new life in Christ. We find the truth of God's Word to help us understand the transition. The Apostle Paul

> *All of us struggle with our old life*

wrote to the Corinthian church, "**Therefore** *if anyone is in Christ, he* *(she) is a new creature; the old things passed away; behold, new things have come."* (2 Corinthians 5:17) Like the butterfly we are a brand-new creature. Our old past of sin has from the memory of God. We are comforted in this in that, *"As far as the east is from the west, far has He removed our transgressions from us.* "(Psalm 103:12) We have a new start from a new birth.

God must do a total make-over of our hearts and minds to be able to use us. When He does change us, He wants us to be useful and productive in His Kingdom plans. Like Jesus' transformation, He wants us to radiate the Light of His Glory.

Much will be required of everyone who has been given much" (Matthew 9:13)

When a person is saved (redeemed, born-again) much has been given to accomplish God's task. He had to give the life of His only Son, Jesus as the sacrifice (atonement) for your sins and mine. A life given for another is a high price and God has high expectations for each of us.

I want to speak to you from a personal level, here. The "much" expected is not unreasonable. In exchange for a new life, there are new expectations. Let me illustrate. My heart transplant resulted in a new life. The new life is difficult for many to understand. I am on new medications, which have different side effects from the ones I took before the transplant.

My diet has not changed, but the preparation has. I can no longer eat at buffets because of the possibility of food contamination by people passing by and leaving their germs everywhere. Fresh, uncooked foods must be thoroughly washed just in case there's a foreign substance on it. Food must be cooked to 165 degrees, no exception. (Even sandwich meat) I cannot attend large functions or travel in airplanes without a protective mask to prevent air-born infections. Why all of this? Because of the anti-rejection medications which significantly lower my immunity. There was a listeria contamination in a local ice cream plant. My nurse told me, "That would make me gravely ill, but it would kill you!"

Life is full of changes and I pray you will never have to experience these conditions, but the fact remains that new life has a deep cost. My deep cost and yours to the new life given by Christ should cause us to want with the depths of our soul to be His and His alone.

Our new life should spark a new light in our lives. All our sins have been forgiven. We have been plucked from death to life by God through His Son, Jesus. In addition, it is now Jesus who lives in us. The new believer has the heart and mind of Christ.

> *"No one has seen God at any time; if we love one another, God abides in us, and His love is perfected in us.* (1 John 4:12)

> *"Blessed be the God and Father of our Lord Jesus Christ, who according to His great mercy has caused us to be born again to a living hope through the resurrection of Jesus Christ from the dead, to obtain an inheritance which is imperishable and undefiled and will not fade away, reserved in heaven for you, who are protected by the power of God through faith for a salvation ready to be revealed in the last time."* (1 Peter 1:3–5)

> *"If we live by the Spirit, let us also walk by the Spirit."* (Galatians 5:25)

We have been called to live a holy life before God. This is only possibility by the indwelling presence of the Holy Spirit. It is the presence of God in us that provides the Light by which we can live in Him and for Him.

The presence of Light within us will naturally want us to share this marvelous new life with every living person we meet. This response becomes as natural as desiring food, water or sleep. The saved person has the indwelling Spirit of the Lord within them and He sparks this deep desire to share His love. This response is not a natural response, but a super-natural response.

God deposits within us a His Spirit of compassion. This is the same compassion Jesus displayed while ministering on earth. Throughout the Old and New Testaments, God's character of compassion has been the standard for the answer to all people's suffering.

God's compassion is especially focused on the hurting and the suffering, whether the people belong to Him or not.

> *"For he will deliver the needy when he cries for help, the afflicted also, and him who has no helper. He will have compassion on the poor and needy, and the lives of the needy he will save. He will rescue their life from oppression and violence, and their blood will be precious in his sight;"* (Psalm 72:12–14)

> *"For as high as the heavens are above the earth, so great is His lovingkindness toward those who fear Him. As far as the east is from the west, so far has He removed our transgressions from us. Just as a father has compassion on his children, so the LORD has compassion on those who fear Him. For He Himself knows our frame; He is mindful that we are but dust.* (Psalm 103:11–14)

The Lord Jehovah God knows everything about us, how weak we are, how we suffer and how people treat us. He knows our sins and choses to "remove our transgressions" from us. This shows us how ready God is in restoring our fellowship with Him. God's compassion is like that of a providing, loving and merciful father. How many times have we disappointed our parents and yet the mark of a loving parent is not to remain aware of all the ways we have failed them. The Psalmist knew how he had sinned and yet in the mercy of the Lord, He still loved them.

The attitude of heart-felt compassion is necessary for the believer to live, work and minister in their marketplace. Jesus first demonstrated compassion. The word compassion means to see the predicament of a person and feel their hurt and despair. When one has compassion, one has the heart of God and Jesus within them.

The opposite of compassion is apathy or indifference. One can see the anguish and pain of another, turn and walk away without offering any assistance. This negative compassion can be attributed in those who claim to follow Jesus as the lack of a genuine Spirit of God filling.

We have too many examples in the New Testament to show Jesus' compassion:

In Mark's Gospel, chapter 8, Jesus had preached to a crowd of 4000. This was the customary 21st Century sermon because it lasted 4 days. Jesus understood the need of people, He wasn't immune to their pain or physical needs and always sought to give them relief. In the passage, Jesus fed the hungry people.

> *"'I feel compassion for the people because they have remained with Me now three days and have nothing to eat. If I send them away hungry to their homes, they will faint on the way; and some of them have come from a great distance.'"* (Mark 8:2–3)

Jesus saw a man named Matthew working the tax collector's booth. Jesus commanded Matthew follow Him. Later that evening Jesus reclined at the dinner table with a group of tax collectors, including Matthew. The Pharisees noticed this event and inquired into the reason why Jesus associated with sinners. Jesus responded, *"But* when Jesus heard this, He said, 'It is not those who are healthy who need a physician, but those who are sick.'" Then Jesus gave them an answer that identified the Pharisees' true heart. He said, 'But go and learn what this means: 'I DESIRE COMPASSION, AND NOT SACRIFICE,' for I did not come to call the righteous, but sinners.'"* (Matthew 9:9-12)

Later in the same chapter, you can see…

"Jesus was going through all the cities and villages, teaching in their synagogues and proclaiming the gospel of the kingdom, and healing every kind of disease and every kind of sickness. Seeing the people, He felt compassion for them, because they were distressed and dispirited like sheep without a shepherd." (Matthew 9:35–36)

These examples are just the tip of the iceberg. There was account after account of the tearing heart of our Savior for the pain and misery of the people.

The Apostle Paul, as the Apostle unto the Gentiles had Jesus' indwelling spirit of compassion. He instructed the church at Colossae,

"So, as those who have been chosen of God, holy and beloved, put on a heart of compassion, kindness, humility, gentleness and patience; bearing with one another, and forgiving each other, whoever has a complaint against anyone; just as the Lord forgave you, so also should you. Beyond all these things put on love, which is the perfect bond of unity. Let the peace of Christ rule in your hearts, to which indeed you were called in one body; and be thankful. Let the word of Christ richly dwell within you, with all wisdom teaching and admonishing one another with psalms and hymns and spiritual songs, singing with thankfulness in your

hearts to God. Whatever you do in word or deed, do all in the name of the Lord Jesus, giving thanks through Him to God the Father." (Colossians 3:12–17)

Notice, we as those chosen (redeemed or saved) by God, should put on a compassionate heart accompanied by kindness, humility, gentleness and patience. These character qualities are essential to live in the Kingdom of God. We want to take our call to salvation seriously and, "Let my light shine before men in such a way that they may see my good works and glorify my Father who is in heaven." (Matthew 5:16) Notice, I have personalized this passage by substituting Paul's "your" with "my".

> *The redeemed of God should put on a compassionate heart accompanied by kindness, humility gentleness and patience*

Once we get out of the comfort of our air-conditioned pews and comfortable surroundings and venture out into the rest of the world, we will see pain and agony that you might say is unimaginable. Let me mention some experiences.

I have witness several life-times the amount of suffering most people in the communities or churches see. Some are horrible, others are sad, but they are all in need of Jesus' compassion. Sometimes all we can give them is Jesus "with skin on" (ourselves).

While in seminary in New Orleans, Louisiana, we often ministered on the river or in the park. We would take sandwiches and cold-drinks and strike up conversations with skid row people. These were people who ran away from a bad home situation in which there was no hope. All these people slept on hard, cold concrete without roofs and the aid of heat or air-conditioning.

We also worked in the gay section of New Orleans. There were times we would visit a home and a person answered the door and said the person we were there to see wasn't feeling well and we'd pray for them. The next week when we returned, we found the person we were there to see wasn't there, possibly due to advanced condition of AIDS or even death.

A team of men have gone into some of our men's prisons and conducted spiritual growth weekends. The first reality that you're no longer in Kansas, Toto, is the clanking of steel doors behind you. Entering some prisons is better than others. Most prisons in Texas are high security. There are more steel bars than you can imagine. Inmates are secluded in small 6 foot by 4 or 5-foot cells, two per cell. They are told when to go, where to go and how to go. There life is a very regimented life, without privacy, frills or freedom.

One weekend we ministered in a prison unit that was preparing inmates for release. There was much more freedom. One learns one is not there to question why an inmate's there or go into your own private life. However, as I sat in front of three inmates in a worship service, I heard one of them say they had been in prison for 20 years. I was dumbfounded. The man looked like he was in his mid-30's or early 40's. I asked him his age and he said, "40 something." The longer I sat there the more I wept. The man had spent half of his life behind bars.

I began to sense a deep compassion for these men. Yes, they were having to pay the penalty for their crimes, but they are still human-beings with feelings, longings, hurts and despair.

There are too many experiences to share now, but one more example. While residing on the transplant unit the nurses and doctors would occasionally ask me to go and visit another patient. I could only say the transplant staff saw the Light of Jesus within me as the reason why they asked in the first place. I thought I had it bad, being a prisoner of an ICU unit with more IV tubes than and old television, but when I saw others, my heart broke into a million pieces. There was one man confined to his bed for the past year. Some had to have a temporary heart pump installed to keep them alive until transplant could occur. Emotions ran high and many awaiting their new life couldn't understand why it was taking so long. My only response was to hold their hand, hug them and as a fellow waiting recipient, I would pray for them and return to visit as their doctors allowed.

Even now, 3 years post-transplant, I find God has exponentially increased my compassion for others. I have seen suffering and experienced some, but the looks on peoples' faces, the depression in their spirit and their deep need for God's intervention can show you what Jesus saw and felt.

My wife, Karen, has commented when I have watched commercials or shows, "I have never seen a grown man cry over kitty cats!" That's new in my life and at first, I asked God, "Why did you give me this curse?" Genuine compassion for people can be painful. Then one day I felt the Holy Spirit saying, "I have given this to you to help you minister to more people and to see the depths of their pain." I can only bear witness that I thanked God for His new compassion in my life and asked to keep it.

This compassion is part of the reason for this book. I sense the Lord leading me to do it for over 1 year and one day I started. There were many self-imposed interruptions to pray and meditate on what I sensed God wanting to say in this work.

Anyone walking in the Light as Jesus walks in the light will see what I am talking about. Walking in God's light or truth, renders a person sensitive to the Holy Spirit's leading and prompting. Walking in the Light will require us all to await God's interruptions so we can share the light. That is the purpose of the church!

We are servants of the Living God. He is our Master. The Apostle Paul knew and communicated this truth many times. (Romans 1:1; 2 Corinthians 4:5; Galatians 1:10; Philippians 1:1; Titus 1:1; James 1:1;

> *The redeemed are servants of the Living God, our Master*

2 Peter 2:1; Jude 1; and Revelation 1:1) Each reference to "bond-servant" is a person who is bearing witness that they have voluntarily sold themselves into the bondage of Jesus Christ. The ultimate self-imposed bond-servant was Jesus. The Apostle Paul shared this truth was a loving and maturing church at Philippi. He said,

> *"Do nothing from selfishness or empty conceit, but with humility of mind regard one another as more important than yourselves; do not merely look out for your own personal interests, but also for the interests of others. Have this attitude in yourselves which was also in Christ Jesus, who, although He existed in the form of God, did not regard equality with God a thing to be grasped, but emptied Himself, taking the form of a bond-servant, and being made in the likeness of men. Being found in appearance as a man, He humbled Himself by becoming obedient to the point of death, even death on a cross. For this reason, also, God highly exalted Him, and bestowed on Him the name which is above every name, so that at the name of Jesus EVERY KNEE WILL BOW, of those who are in heaven and on earth and under the earth,"* (Philippians 2:3–10)

Paul knew Jesus had taken the form of a bond-servant, one under the orders and authority of another, our Heavenly Father. Jesus surrendered Himself to the task at hand, which had been prepared before the beginning of time. Because of his surrender Jesus didn't constantly think "How Great I Am", but instead thought of Himself as a man to identify with our sins and weaknesses, without Himself sinning.

> *Walking in the Light means our care for others is of supreme importance*

We are being re-made in the imagine of Jesus. This process is an on-going one. There are some things we must do that Jesus will not do for us.

"For everyone who exalts himself will be humbled, and he who humbles himself will be exalted." (Luke 14:11)

"humble yourselves under the mighty hand of God, that He may exalt you at the proper time, casting all your anxiety on Him, because He cares for you." (1 Peter 5:6–7)

The key thought here is we must humble ourselves. No one else can do it for us. It means to "make low". We have a great need to lower the opinions of ourselves, our importance, our professions and our status within the body of Christ or the world. Instead we are expected by God to consider first, others.

When a person walks in God's light, the care for others is of supreme importance and drive. That passion becomes as normal as breathing itself. When we witness brutalities upon others, such as we have seen in the past decade, a Light filled person will naturally have the response of God Almighty coursing within their veins. I am not speaking of revenge or death to the agents of misery, but compassion upon their victims and a desire to intercede with prayers and ministry to them.

When Hurricane Harvey battered Houston in 2017 the historic flood waters covered areas that the Gulf Coast of Texas with levels of flooding never before seen. Houston is use to flooding rains and hurricanes, but not like Harvey.

People from all over the United States responded. Work, nearly a year later is still on-going. Teams from churches throughout the South and all parts of North American filled Houston with their compassionate love and help. We witnessed the communities coming together, too. People helped people they didn't know with rescuing them from the quickly rising waters, food, shelter, clean-up and repair.

We, in Houston, often complain about the "I don't give a hoot about others" attitude, but Harvey brought Houston and Texas together. Witnessing ministry in action was so heartbreakingly warming and we knew the Spirit of the Living God was alive and well.

The attitude displayed during this catastrophe is precisely the compassion Jesus displayed in His ministry. Not all people work for the same reason, but compassion for hurting people is a Christ-like response.

> *"And two blind men sitting by the road, hearing that Jesus was passing by, cried out, 'Lord, have mercy on us, Son of David!' The crowd sternly told them to be quiet, but they cried out all the more, 'Lord, Son of David, have mercy on us!' And Jesus stopped and called them, and said, 'What do you want Me to do for you?' They said to Him, 'Lord, we want our eyes to be opened.' Moved with compassion, Jesus touched their eyes; and immediately they regained their sight and followed Him."* (Matthew 20:30–34)

> *"And a leper came to Jesus, beseeching Him and falling on his knees before Him, and saying, 'If You are willing, You can make me clean.' Moved with compassion, Jesus stretched out His hand and touched him, and said to him, 'I am willing; be cleansed.' Immediately the leprosy left him and he was cleansed."* (Mark 1:40–42)

> **God shows Himself to those walking in the Light of His Son Jesus**

> *"Now as He approached the gate of the city, a dead man was being carried out, the only son of his mother, and she was a widow; and a sizeable crowd from the city was with her.*
>
> *When the Lord saw her, He felt compassion for her, and said to her, 'Do not weep.' And He came up and touched the coffin; and the bearers came to a halt. And He said, 'Young man, I say to you, arise!' The dead man sat up and began to speak. And Jesus gave him back to his mother. Fear gripped them all, and they began glorifying God, saying, 'A great prophet has arisen among us!' and, 'God has visited His people!" This report concerning Him went out all over Judea and in all the surrounding district.* (Luke 7:12–17)

The key truth in these passages was faith in those who sought Jesus' help and their faith that made their request possible. Every person has many opportunities to submit to Jesus, but only those who walk in the light do so regularly because they hear His voice and know His heart.

Indeed, God visits His people. This fact does not have to be the exception, but rather an on-going truth. God shows Himself to those who are walking in the light of His Son, Jesus. He shows Himself for four reasons. First, He wants you to know His great love for you. Secondly, He wants you to get to know Him intimately and as you obey and follow Him you are able to know God by experience. Third, God wants to call you to be on mission with Him and this is how you see Him work and your admiration and dedication grows further. Fourth, He wants to transform you into the image of His Son, Jesus.

The temptation I have witnessed people facing is they don't believe God can change a person like me. That's where you are absolutely wrong! You may think the way you've previously lived your life makes it impossible for God to change and use you. There are two examples within the Scriptures that disprove your idea. First was David, King of Israel. David saw a beautiful woman, Beersheba, whom he deeply lusted to have. He conspired to have Beersheba's husband sent to a battle in which David was sure he would die. The husband was killed and David took Beersheba. The prophet Nathan confronted David in his sin and David repented. God's Word describes David's life after repentance as, "A man after God's own heart." (Acts 13:22)

The second example in Scriptures was Saul, later renamed by God as Paul. After the founding of the church in Jerusalem, Saul became a serious persecutor of the Christians. As a member of the Pharisees, Saul felt compelled to uphold the teachings and traditions of the Jewish people. We are shown in Acts 7:60 at the stoning of Stephen.

> *Saul was in hearty agreement with putting him to death. And on that day a great persecution began against the church in Jerusalem, and they were all scattered throughout the regions of Judea and Samaria, except the apostles. Some devout men buried Stephen, and made loud lamentation over him. But Saul began ravaging the church, entering house after house, and dragging off men and women, he would put them in prison.* (Acts 8:1–3)

In Acts 9, the author of Acts recorded an encounter Saul had that radically changed his life.

> *"As he was traveling, it happened that he was approaching Damascus, and <u>suddenly a light from heaven flashed around him</u>; and he fell to the ground and heard a voice saying to him, 'Saul, Saul, why are you persecuting Me?' And he said, 'Who are You, Lord?' And He said, 'I am Jesus whom you are persecuting, but get up and enter the city, and it will be told you what you must do.' The men who traveled with him stood speechless, hearing the voice but seeing no one. Saul*

> *got up from the ground, and though his eyes were open, he could see nothing; and leading him by the hand, they brought him into Damascus. And he was three days without sight, and neither ate nor drank.* (Acts 9:3–9)

Notice, "suddenly a light from heaven flashed around him". The Light of Christ appeared and changed Saul's life. In Acts 13:9 Saul became known as Paul, a new man, a new name and a new attitude toward Christ. From the time of the "light encounter" on, Paul was known as the Apostle unto the Gentiles. Paul's life was changed from a persecutor of the church to a man who planted or started many churches, constantly traveling and strengthening and correcting false doctrine within the church.

Please dispel your belief that God cannot use you because of your background or who you are right now. He will transform you by the power of His will and Word. The fact is always present that God want you to know Him more intimately today than you did yesterday. As we come to know Him, our love for Him grows and our obedience grows.

> *A Disciple-making ministry is essential to lead people to walk in the Light*

Give yourself a chance. There will be a lot of distractions presented to you by people around you, such as: family, friends and maybe even people in church. Let me encourage you, listen to only one voice, the voice of the Lord God Almighty. He is the only One that holds your eternity in His hands. Others may tempt you away from your devoted life in Christ, but the Father will always be drawing you, encouraging you, empowering you and loving you.

Please walk in His light. There is life in the light. Personally, all the folks I've known that have completely surrendered their lives to

Him, live in a great joy.

You may have been trained as a fire-fighter, a soldier, a CPA or a hair dresser, but the most important training an individual can receive is how to follow the Lord. Again, in the Great Commission, (Matthew 28:18-20) the church is given the responsibility of making disciples (that is you and I) by teaching people all that Jesus taught on earth. This is a massive undertaking because ministers encounter people that refuse to be taught for various reasons. But the truth remains, it is our ministry and job to teach people how to follow Jesus.

Through the years of leading a discipleship ministry, as Pastor, I have been blessed to see people who once stood in the spectators' seats of the church's ministry come alive. I have witnessed people finally crossing the line of indecision about surrendering to Christ in salvation saved. I have witnessed Senior Adults come alive and instead of sitting in the pews, coming alive and with a great deal of excitement becoming active witnesses and ministering to their community. Next, we will examine this ministry given by Christ, empowered by the Holy Spirit and glorifying the Heavenly Father. Ready?

<u>Disciple-making process</u> (Discipleship, Member Training)

Another fundamental truth in walking in the Light is a long-term disciple-training ministry. This is not a program. It is not a function. It is not a passive ministry. What I mean by passive is the disciple (you) is not sitting in a pew absorbing a bunch of material. I have found people that begin with "oh, well" and soon become truly excited. They are coming to know God in a personal encounter with Him as they study the Word. Their lives are anchored to Jesus. They are no longer tossed about by every passing wind of religious thought.

> *"And He gave some as apostles, and some as prophets, and some as evangelists, and some as pastors and teachers, for the equipping of the saints for the work of service, to the building up of the body of Christ; until we all attain to the unity of the faith, and of the knowledge of the Son of God, to a mature man, to the measure of the stature which belongs to the fullness of Christ. As a result, we are no longer to be children, tossed here and there by waves and carried about by every wind of doctrine, by the trickery of men, by craftiness in deceitful scheming; but speaking the truth in love, we are to grow up in all aspects into Him who is the head, even Christ, from whom the whole body, being fitted and held together by what every joint supplies, according to the proper working of each individual part, causes the growth of the body for the building up of itself in love.*
> (Ephesians 4:11–16)

The same Paul that had earlier persecuted the church lovingly and prophetically wrote this in his letter to the Ephesian church. There are several key aspects of this passage:

1. God gave us, the people a great gift: "the apostles, and some as prophets, and some as evangelists, and some as pastors and teachers," (Verse 11)

2. The function of the apostle, prophets, evangelist, pastors and teachers to build each of us up "for the work of service" (Verse 12)

    - Notice here is a deeply important understanding for the 21st Century church.
    - We are being groomed, prepared and trained for "works of service" not sitting on the sidelines.

3. "until we all attain to the unity of the faith, and of the knowledge of the Son of God, to a mature man, to the measure of the stature which belongs to the fullness of Christ" (Verse 13)

- Unity is so often misunderstood and applied in modern churches, but it simply means we are all here to work to glorify the One God.

- Unity means we recognize we all have the same God-given vision about our church's ministry and our participation within those ministries.

- Unity doesn't mean we're all doing the same jobs or doing them the same way or we are a bunch of mindless robots functioning like machines,

- It does mean we use our specifically given spiritual gifts, as parts of the whole body of Christ to accomplish our God-given vision and ministry.

Ladies think of it this way. You have assembled the ingredients for a cake or pie. I am not an epicurean, so I will not insult you in my instructions, but there is a lesson here. I do know there is sometimes an order in which one adds ingredients. You bake it and then you enjoy it. The lessons is that it takes many different ingredients to make a yummy pie or cake. You don't have on your dining room table a bowl of flour, a container of flavoring, a bucket of sugar and various ingredients for a person to take a little of each ingredient to put in their mouth and expect it to taste like the expected cake or pie. Everything has to work together. So do the spiritual gifts. we each are gifted differently but work to the same function: worshipping the

Father, ministering to the saints and our community, evangelizing the lost, discipling the body and to having fun and laughter while working together.

Brothers and sister in Christ, there are so many ways I can approach this subject for you. Cooking might be your passion. Hunting, fishing, camping or the outdoors may be your enjoyment or even tinkering with mechanical things. The same truth applies that all the things you use, all the training and practice you invest in, all the tools you might use all have one ultimate desired outcome. Like the recipe about, we each are gifted differently but work to the same function: worship the Father, ministering to the saints and our community, evangelizing the lost, discipling the body and to having fun and laughter while working together.

The disciple-making ministry is so important. Think of the disciples. How long did they walk with Jesus before He turned them loose? How long was the Apostle Paul in the disciple-making process? Many think Paul instantly knew everything. There are two fallacies about this. First, no one is mature enough to instantly know the truths of Christ. Secondly, we know from Scriptures both Paul (Galatians 1:18) and the disciples were trained for 3 years. How long do most ministers train in seminary? 3 years.

The disciple-making process is quite detailed. There is classroom work. Jesus used a quiet mountainside classroom. There is also learning on the go. As two people walk side-by-side, talk, pray and study Scriptures learning can occur. A disciple is defined as a student sitting and learning from a master. There are some hyper-righteous people who believe that the Holy Spirit imparts all they need to know. Well that is partially true. The Holy Spirit does teach, but initially a student needs to learn from an older Christian.

Another facet of this diamond is there are truths that we need to learn from others experience. We need to learn doctrine. The Light

Walker needs to learn how to pray, effectively and with power. The Light Walker must learn to witness, minister and eventually become a leader in the church. All of this does not come from osmosis, diffusion or simply standing under an apple tree during harvest season. It is intentional and purposeful.

Through the years of pastoring I have been given the responsibility of discipling churches and specific individuals. I have discovered that people that have a passion for being discipled make great example, effective ministers, themselves and can function beautifully maintaining the purpose of the church. Those who most often refuse to be discipled have been the ones I have experienced great problems from.

How many of you have been trained to do funerals? How many feel they have been sufficiently trained to make hospital visits? There are medical protocols to watch out for. Then there are subjects and discussions one should avoid during the visit. These skills need sensitivity and God's grace.

Let me illustrate what I'm talking about. Suppose you go into a room and the loving brother in the bed said they've found throat cancer and they want to immediately do surgery. I have heard stories from people making visits that they told the patient about how their Aunt had that surgery and the doctors removed everything from the jawbone to their shoulder and there was a chasm of stuff showing. <u>Believe me do not do this</u>!!! You are probably saying, "I know better." Not everyone does or there wouldn't be this story. Good intentions does not make good ministry.

Discipleship is a classroom event, a field training and a private time with a mentor. I have discipled people that have been a Christian for decades. They often ask, "Why hasn't anyone taken the time to do this for me before?" I have an answer, but you think about it.

Next, we need to discuss the relationship of walking in the Light and prayer. *Jesus said, "And*

> *He said to them, 'It is written, MY HOUSE SHALL BE CALLED A HOUSE OF PRAYER; but you are making it a ROBBERS' DEN."* (Matthew 21:13)

Most people would admit they aren't conducting commerce like the money changers were in Jesus' day, but within the past few years we haven't noticed much prayer in most churches. Over the past several years I have been able to see the patterns of churches. The day of the corporate prayer meeting is gone! How sad.

Corporate prayer time has been replaced with prayer chapels (good idea) and call-in prayer lines (slightly ok). The body of Christ needs the power and unity of corporate prayer. Oh, we're too busy? We're too busy to spend quality time talking to the Father in a corporate prayer meeting? What a shame and how these churches are losing out on the power of God.

When I look at the vitality of a church the first thing I want to know about is corporate prayer time. The lack of corporate prayer time usually has a directly proportional success in evangelism, discipleship, ministry and future leadership building.

Corporate Prayer

I have found people Walking in the Light want corporate prayer opportunities with a deep hunger and thirst. Yes, it may be a bit old-fashioned, but if this is the case, so is worship, Sunday School and Ladies' Tea.

New church starts sometimes catches the ole' school off guard. We were beginning a new church in Florida and our schedule did not match any of our modern-day traditional or too many of the contemporary churches. This was our schedule:

<u>Sunday morning</u>

   9:00 a.m.   Discipleship classes

  10:30 a.m.   Fellowship time

  11:00 a.m.   Worship

<u>Some week night</u> - depending on the group's preference

6:00 p.m. Fellowship time (often a pot-luck dinner) and gathering for prayer

7:00 p.m.ish   Bible study

7:30 p.m. Prayer time

The reason why I have given you this is to see my seriousness about corporate prayer. It is the time of empowerment for evangelism and missions. Prayer brings the hearts of the redeemed into unity and we can effectively pray for the sick, the lost and the disenfranchised. Corporate prayer also brings a sweet flavor to the body of Christ and we can share our problems, difficulties and struggles with each other around tables.

> *"These all with one mind were continually devoting themselves to prayer, along with the women, and Mary the mother of Jesus, and with His brothers."* (Acts 1:14)

> *"They were continually devoting themselves to the apostles' teaching and to fellowship, to the breaking of bread and to prayer. Everyone kept feeling a sense of awe; and many wonders and signs were taking place through the apostles. And all those who had believed were together and had all things in common; and they began selling their property and possessions and were sharing them with all, as anyone might have need.*

Day by day continuing with one mind in the temple, and breaking bread from house to house, they were taking their meals together with gladness and sincerity of heart, praising God and having favor with all the people. And the Lord was adding to their number day by day those who were being saved." (Acts 2:42–47)

What do you see that is unique here?

- Twice Dr. Luke tells us the Jerusalem church "devoted themselves to prayer"
- They were dedicated to the teaching of the Apostles
- They were loyal to fellowshipping with each other (breaking of bread)

Now, I ask what was the result?
- They possessed one mind (unity)
- There was great joy
- They had Spirit-filled worship
- Miraculously, "the Lord was adding to their number day by day those who were being saved."

Do you think these efforts are worth it? They did. So why are we finding more and more churches short-sheeting their church members and the Lord? Is it expedience of time? Lack of interest in the body of Christ?

My experiences indicate a lot of people within our churches want more than they're receiving. They know that prayer and discipleship are marks of obedience. They are also issues of true spiritual health. People are hungering and thirsting for more of Christ. They're tired of Info-sermons which teach theoretical Christianity and want real meat. This is a situation not cured by the Balm in Gilead. It is cured by obedience to the Light.

Thom Rainer, President and CEO of Lifeway Christian ministries said,

- "We should not confuse routine, perfunctory prayer for dynamic, corporate prayer.
- When we pray, we should pray for not only physical needs but for spiritual ones as well.
- Dynamic corporate prayer is when God's people come together to intercede to God for specific needs in the church.
- Review the prayer in your church. Is it possible people are just going through the motions with prayer?"

Prayer is not a program, an activity, a time slot in the weekly church calendar or a few minutes of one's day, it is the life coursing through the veins of a believer. Prayer is a way of life. Prayer is our conversation, our relationship and the direction for our lives and ministries from God Almighty.

> ***Prayer is not a program***

Walking in the Light and ministering

The Light idea of ministering occurs within the body of Christ and within the community. Some churches have blessed "home-bound" ministries and deacon ministries. Others are struggling with how to get people involved and provide life-blessing ministry to people.

There are two types of ministry. The first is to the body of Christ and the second is to the community surrounding the church. There are several key elements in common: compassion or love for people, a deep desire to eliminate suffering and enriching their lives by the presence of the Lord. The final key element is we are glorifying the Lord God.

There are so many misconceptions about Community missions. I have been accused more than once of being a socialist or communist. My response has been, "I'm only following Jesus' example. He must have been a socialist or communist, too!"

There is a crucial difference between church ministry and socialism or communism. In church ministry it comes from obedience to the Lord Jesus Himself. No one is under obligation. Everything is voluntary as the Spirit moves. In the socialist/communist people are forced to give up their possessions or something similar. Believe me I'm not an expert here, but I know what I've seen in the days of the Cold War. One shares their good out of obligation, the other has everything taken from the people and held by the state. Jesus never forces anyone to do anything they, themselves do not want to do. He moves and should the people be receptive to the Holy Spirit, they respond.

Ministry done out of love is Jesus' "compassion in action" (CIA). Sometimes churches within a community have reputations. Hopefully they have the reputation of caring and loving like Jesus, but sometimes through the years people forget why their church exist. They may grow attitudes of insiders only, a fraternal or sorority of believers.

Jesus will shine His light upon your life and the life of your church. Those that have spiritual eyes and ears will see and hear what Jesus is saying. You will have to prayerfully discern what He is saying about your expression of love in ministry through the Holy Spirit.

The E.R. ministry (more details in Appendix 1) became a regular weekly event. Our church body loved providing this ministry and they learned about dealing with people of every culture, religion and socio-economic background. The recipients of the ministry seemed to find encouragement from our visits.

The financial expense of ministry is usually insignificant. Sometimes the body of Christ begins ministries by providing the resources themselves. Many times, churches begin budgeting or talking special community missions offerings to fund the ministry.

Have you ever asked or heard someone else ask, "How much will it cost?" Unfortunately, this attitude shows the wrong motive and possibly even a heart not centered in Christ. The more important question to ask is, "What will it cost if I (we) don't respond to God's invitation to do this ministry?" Remember the example I shared about the Parable of the Talents? (Matthew 25)

What did the two servants who did their master's will experience?

12 OUR ONENESS IN THE LIGHT

"I do not ask on behalf of these alone, but for those also who believe in Me through their word; that they may all be one; even as You, Father, are in Me and I in You, that they also may be in Us, so that the world may believe that You sent Me." (John 17:20–21)

There are many words that are synonymous with unity: oneness, agreement, harmony, accord and unison. The biblical truth is that one has the same mind, the same heart and the same mission.

The idea of a oneness or unity for us on earth does not interfere with our individual personalities, or abilities. God has created us all to be individuals with different personalities, different spiritual gifts, different abilities and possibilities. It is this individualism which gives us different perspectives about any given subject. For example, the Gospels of the New Testament were penned by men under the inspiration of the Holy Spirit.

Each Gospel records similar events but from different perspectives. Matthew's Gospel account of Jesus' birth is from the Jewish perspective. Matthew records Jesus' ancestral genealogy and includes the announcement by the angel to Joseph. The angel disclosed to Joseph the name the child was to be given, Jesus. (Matthew 1)

Luke's Gospel was written to a generally Gentile audience rather than Jewish. Gentiles were all other people groups outside of the Israelites and God's Covenant. This Gospel account discloses to Mary and not Joseph what was about to happen. Luke was a Gentile physician and therefore wrote from the Gentile perspective.

Should you decide to test our individualism, take a passage of Scripture and ask two different people of different backgrounds to study it, from the same resources and then teach it. You will notice many similarities, but also God inspiring the different personalities with different emphasis. This is perfectly normal.

Unity includes our individualism plus extra God-given elements. These God-given components of the individual is due to one vital truth expressed by the Apostle Paul:

> *"Therefore I, the prisoner of the Lord, implore you to walk in a manner worthy of the calling with which you have been called, with all humility and gentleness, with patience, showing tolerance for one another in love, being diligent to preserve the unity of the Spirit in the bond of peace. There is <u>one body</u> and <u>one Spirit</u>, just as also you were called in <u>one hope</u> of your calling; <u>one Lord</u>, <u>one faith</u>, <u>one baptism</u>, <u>one God and Father of all who is over all and through all and in all</u>."* (Ephesians 4:1–6)

I have underlined part of Ephesians 4:1-6 to show you where unity originates. The phrase "one body" refers to the body of Christ, or the church. In our modern-day society, we see different churches, different denominations and slightly different beliefs. But Paul is speaking of the Bride of Christ, the one church, or the church-universal. Unless your Bible has more chapters in the book of Revelation than mine, there will not be a Baptist Heaven, a Catholic Heaven, an Assembly of God Heaven, a Pentecostal Heaven, A Nazarene Heaven or any other segregation of peoples. We will be one people praising God the Father and the Lord Jesus Christ, His Son. Paul is saying the truth of the "one body" is unifying or bonds us together.

The "One Spirit" refers to the one Holy Spirit. There is not a different Spirit from denomination to denomination or from the Old Testament (Spirit of the Lord) to the New Testament (the Holy Spirit). There is but one and only one Holy Spirit and He is the same Spirit indwelling all genuine followers of Jesus. This common thread in us all leads the whole body of believers in all churches and denominations to live according to God's Word. The One Spirit inspire us all, each according to the will and wishes of God to do that which He has purposed for us.

The One Holy Spirit is the same Spirit that lives in Jesus' followers in Africa, Europe, Asia, South America, North America, Antarctica and under the deepest sea and on the highest mountain. In John's Gospel Jesus mentions the "Spirit" 23 times in 18 verses. John's Gospel has the most descriptions of the Holy Spirit.

John 1:32-33	The Holy Spirit descended upon Jesus at His baptism.

John 3:5–7	*"Jesus answered, 'Truly, truly, I say to you, unless one is born of water and the Spirit he cannot enter into the kingdom of God. That which is born of the flesh is flesh, and that which is born of the Spirit is spirit. Do not be amazed that I said to you, 'You must be born again."*

John 14:16–18	*"I will ask the Father, and He will give you another Helper, that He may be with you forever; that is the Spirit of truth, whom the world cannot receive, because it does not see Him or know Him, but you know Him because He abides with you and will be in you. I will not leave you as orphans; I will come to you."*

John 14:26	*"But the Helper, the Holy Spirit, whom the Father will send in My name, He will teach you all things, and bring to your remembrance all that I said to you.*

John 20:19-23	*A short time after Jesus' resurrection He appeared to the disciples. And when He had said this, He showed them both His hands and His side. The disciples then rejoiced when they saw the Lord. So Jesus said to them again, "Peace be with you; as the Father has sent Me, I also send you."*

> *And when He had said this, He breathed on them and said to them, "Receive the Holy Spirit. "If you forgive the sins of any, their sins have been forgiven them; if you retain the sins of any, they have been retained."*

You will notice when Jesus breathed on them, "inspired them,", which filled the disciples with the Holy Spirit, Jesus also empowered them to continue His ministry. There is an additional time when this Divine filling came, in Acts 1:4-5:

> *Gathering them together, He commanded them not to leave Jerusalem, but to wait for what the Father had promised, "Which," He said, "you heard of from Me; for John baptized with water, but you will be baptized with the Holy Spirit not many days from now."*

Later, on the day of Pentecost this event occurred and fulfilled the prophecy of Jesus.

> *"When the day of Pentecost had come, they were all together in one place. And suddenly there came from heaven a noise like a violent rushing wind, and it filled the whole house where they were sitting. And there appeared to them tongues as of fire distributing themselves, and they rested on each one of them. And they were all filled with the Holy Spirit and began to speak with other tongues, as the Spirit was giving them utterance.* (Acts 2:1–4)

The indwelling of the Holy Spirit, the Spirit of the Living God, is what has transformed people into the image of Jesus throughout the centuries since Jesus' ascension into Heaven. Today the Holy Spirit still transforms people into the image of Jesus, teaches us, reminds us, encourages us and convicts us of sin. The presence of the Holy Spirit in those who are born again is what enables us and empowers us to walk in the Light.

"One hope" is the next phrase in Ephesians 4:1-6. The word "hope" signifies something in which we look forward to or something we "live for". People have always lived in a fallen world. Believers are referred to as "aliens" (Acts 7:6; 1 Peter 1:1; 2:11) living in a foreign land.

Let me illustrate my point. Have you ever been in a strange place in which you truly didn't know exactly where you were or you did not know the language and customs? Once while doing church strengthening work in South America I remember how interesting the country was and how colorful the people and their customs were, but I was an alien from North America. I stood out like a dog in a cat farm. One day I remembered, "I sure would like to have a hamburger from home."

This is the realization that you are a foreigner in a strange land. This is precisely the way Christians, who walk in the Light feel. We are here on earth, but where we will truly feel at home is in the presence of God Almighty in Heaven. This is a promise Jesus made in John 14:1-3. He said,

> *"'Do not let your heart be troubled; believe in God, believe also in Me. In My Father's house are many dwelling places; if it were not so, I would have told you; for I go to prepare a place for you. If I go and prepare a place for you, I will come again and receive you to Myself, that where I am, there you may be also.'"*

We, who serve the Light, know we are in a foreign land, growing more foreign by the day. Our aspirations or hope is to one day realize the promise of Jesus and go into the next life to be with Him.

For many people today, they hope for something to happen, but the certainty isn't there. They hope to be financially well off, to open their own business or to get married and have a child. For these people hope is a strong wish, but for Christians hope is a fact waiting to be delivered.

One Lord is the next phrase in Ephesians 4:1-6. The phrase "Lord" has many different meanings. The term "lording it over" leans to an understanding of one in authority over another. It means boss. Here Paul means, The Supernatural Being, the Creator and the Master.

AFTERWORD

"Lighting the Path to God's Presence in You"

The essence of this book is focusing on a personal, intimate walk with Almighty God and Father of Jesus Christ, our Savior.

Many people falsely believe making a profession of faith, baptism and having one's name on a church role is their guarantee of their Heavenly reward. Oh, they may be faithful to attend every meeting, or not. There are tremendous amounts of false beliefs of all kinds that have come into the body of Christ over the past two millennia and much of it is innocent.

There are a few crucial points about Christian faith which is given by Jesus in John's Gospel. Let me briefly summarize these truths.

First, one must accept the fact and truth that God is the Creator of all there is. We do not understand the how He created everything, that is not important, but what is important is the fact that He did create everything. Then we must accept the truth of God, in His Word, that without faith it is impossible to please Him. (Hebrews 11:6)

Secondly, that God loves you and cares for you so much. He wants you to depend upon Him for <u>all</u> your life's needs and know that He is the One who provides them for you. This second truth is the central truth behind the reason why Jesus came to earth. (John 3:16–18)

> *"For God so loved the world, that He gave His only begotten Son, that whoever believes in Him shall not perish, but have eternal life. For God did not send the Son into the world to judge the world, but that the world might be saved through Him. He who believes in Him is not judged; he who does not believe has been judged already, because he has not believed in the name of the only begotten Son of God."*

The third truth is the Deity of Jesus Christ. (John 1:1-5)

John 1:1–5 *The Deity of Jesus Christ*

In the beginning was the Word, and the Word was with God, and the Word was God. He was in the beginning with God. All things came into being through Him, and apart from Him nothing came into being that has come into being. In Him was life, and the life was the Light of men. The Light shines in the darkness, and the darkness did not comprehend it.

Jesus is God from before the beginning of time. He is responsible for all of creation, including you and me. Life itself is contained only in Him. While many accept Jesus' Deity, there are many more who do not. His Light shines in a dark (sinful) world, but it cannot grasp either His deity or purpose, to seek and save the lost. (Luke 19:10)

The fourth truth is, *"And the Word became flesh, and dwelt among us, and we saw His glory, glory as of the only begotten from the Father, full of grace and truth.* (John 1:14) The Truth is a person, not a relative concept. He who was "in the beginning" became a human being just like you and me. God stepped down off His throne to come and identify with humanity, to be tempted in every way as we are and remain the only sinless person born of flesh. (Hebrews 4:15) God came, out of His great love for us, to offer us a restoration or a rebuilding of the relationship He intended before the creation. Jesus came to restore us to a relationship with Almighty God so that we might have a loving relationship and glorify the Heavenly Father.

The fifty truth is, Jesus openly identified His previously hidden identity by saying, *"I am the Light of the world; he who follows Me will not walk in the darkness but will have the Light of life."* (John 8:12) Jesus' revelation or unveiling of His identity publicly identified Him as the LORD of Creation, Jehovah God, or Almighty God. He was and is the Light of the world shedding light upon the truth of God and in doing so, shining light upon our lives so we can see our need for Him in salvation and be able to see the true condition of our lives.

The sixth truth, which is the basis for this book is in John 14:21-

24. Jesus said,

> "'He who has My commandments and keeps them is the one who loves Me; and he who loves Me will be loved by My Father, and I will love him and will disclose Myself to him.' Judas (not Iscariot) said to Him, 'Lord, what then has happened that You are going to disclose Yourself to us and not to the world.' Jesus answered and said to him, 'If anyone loves Me, he will keep My word; and My Father will love him, and We will come to him and make Our abode with him. He who does not love Me does not keep My words; and the word which you hear is not Mine, but the Father's who sent Me.'"

God with us, Immanuel (Jesus) gave us a truth so important every human being should be made aware of its content. Jesus said, "If you love Me, you will obey me." There is no room for gray in the statement of fact. Our love for Jesus is the driving force in our lives to obey Him.

Jesus promised that those who love Him will by loved by the Heavenly Father and Him (Jesus). What more powerful and fulfilling love could there ever be than the love of God for you and me?

Then Jesus gave the second part of the promise, *"I will disclose myself to him."* Jesus promised to reveal Himself or His character, His plans, His purposes and His will to us. In other words, He will make it possible to know Him intimately in ways we could have never known Him before. This disclosure or revelation will cause us to love Him even more and create in us a clean heart and a right standing before God. We will be known as sons and daughters of the Living God.

Jesus makes a final promise, *"We will come to him and make Our abode with him."* If knowing Jesus and the Heavenly Father wasn't enough, Jesus promises that they will come and make their abode (home, residence) in us (you). I can only testify as to the impact this truth has made upon my life. I have loved Jesus for several years, and I have discovered my love has grown immensely over the past decade. I am no longer the same individual. This love has motivated me to be more faithful and dedicated to His service and to you, the reader of this book and God's children in His churches.

I have sensed the presence of Almighty God in my life and where ever I go. As the old American Express commercials use to say, "I don't leave home without Him!" This doesn't mean I am a super-Christian, it only means I attempt to live my life with a single purpose, to glorify Him.

The Lord God lives in our home. He travels in my auto with me. He is present in every second of my life and there in whatever I face, no matter what.

I pray you can discover His presence in your life, too, if you haven't already. Maybe He is appealing you to a specific task, or to get away from a certain lifestyle. Let me encourage you – do not be afraid or put it off. What ever God's calling you to do will have such unimaginable results that you won't want to delay doing it or refusing to do it.

May the LORD God bless you and reveal His great love for you.

Your fellow journey companion,

Bill Jernigan

ABOUT THE AUTHOR

Bill has served as Pastor for over twenty-five years. During his pastorates his God-given passion has been to witness people's spiritual life being revived and filled with the excitement and security of knowing they are a child of The Living God redeemed by His Son, Jesus and given victory over the trials of this life.

He has worked in inner-city missions, international church strengthening and growth. He presently serves as a volunteer on his state's church renewal team, and a volunteer on the heart transplant unit.

He takes seriously Jesus' commandment in Matthew 28:18-20 about going into the world and proclaiming Jesus as the only Savior and making disciples of those who embrace Jesus as Lord and Savior. He has used a long-range disciple making plan for years with a great deal of success and he would be happy to share it with you.

Bill can be reached by email through the ministry website:
www.billjerniganministries.org

Bible Studies Available on the website
"Helping Your Children Become Followers of Christ" is a 5 week study for parents to help Making Disciples of their children based upon Deuteronomy 6.

"Return to Mayberry" is a 6 week study to help the believer make healthy connections within the community to enable them to be able to share their testimony and salvation in their relationships.

"My Two New Hearts" a book written to share a story of a 28 year ordeal with heart failure and how God interceded and provided throughout the years.

FROM THE AUTHOR'S HEART TO YOURS

The Lord God put in my heart many decades, the desire to lead His people to live their lives in His righteousness. I have found this to be a goal the Father has for every redeemed Child. Every person on earth must walk in The Almighty's power, truth and presence.

This ministry goal has certain positives and what some might say are negatives. The positives are easy to see. I have had the blessings of witnessing people have their lives radically changed and once changed they become builders of the Kingdom of God. They are able to participate in the joy of the Lord as they help others see the Light.

The only negative is not everyone wants to live in the Light of the Lord. These people are usually the most vocal and distractive, but once you listen to their complaints, you recognize they aren't from the Lord.

Throughout the years I have tried to teach the Word of God so that it can be easily understood. I have made myself available to talk privately with people in the church seeking solid spiritual questions. Love has been my motive.

Love for God's people is the motive for this book. My prayer is that you are able to catch a glimpse of walking in the Light of Christ, on a personal level. That the Light in you might shine on others and help them walk in the Light of Jesus, too.

You are welcome to contact me if I may be of help to you. You may email me at: bill@billjerniganministries.org. I would be happy to hear from you, always.

NOTES

Chapter 1

[1] Wiersbe, W. W. (1993). *Wiersbe's Expository Outlines on the Old Testament* (Genesis 1). Wheaton, IL: Victor Books.

[2] Henry, M. (1994). *Matthew Henry's commentary on the whole Bible: complete and unabridged in one volume* (p. 5). Peabody: Hendrickson.

[3] Ibid.

[4] Ackendorf, Julie. "How Did Ancient People Use the Stars and Planets?" last modified January 30, 2018. http://sciencing.com/did-people-use-stars-planets-8675019.html

Chapter 2

[1] Jamieson, R., Fausset, A. R., and Brown, D. (1997). *Commentary Critical and Explanatory on the Whole Bible* (Vol. 1, p. 383). Oak Harbor, WA: Logos Research Systems, Inc.

[2] Henry, M. (1994). *Matthew Henry's commentary on the whole Bible: complete and unabridged in one volume* (p. 1699). Peabody: Hendrickson.

[3] Ibid

Chapter 6

[1] Blum, E. A. (1985). John. In J. F. Walvoord and R. B. Zuck (Eds.), *The Bible Knowledge Commentary: An Exposition of the Scriptures* (Vol. 2, p. 303). Wheaton, IL: Victor Books.

Chapter 8

[1] Wiersbe, W. W. (1996). *The Bible exposition commentary* (Vol. 2, p. 389).Wheaton, IL: Victor Books.

APPENDIX 1

Suggestions on Shining Your Light in Community

Community Mission Ideas for your church

Read Matthew 25: 31-46

Some thoughts are in-house, but a great deal of research and response have shown that a large majority of people will not come to the "church" but the church can go to the people in market-place, off-site ministry locations. There ministry can occur, Bible study classes can be conducted and people can have an opportunity to find the Jesus that "went to the well, went to the wedding, went from town to town healing the deformed and ill.

These ministries are ideas only. Some ministries are done among the body of Christ and others are done within the community to show the love of Jesus. Ministry shouldn't be done with the attitude and goal of "gaining members". Ministry is done because you love Jesus and want to obey Him and because you love your neighbor and want to express your love for them and provide a witness of the saving grace only through Jesus.

I am convinced, convicted and strongly committed to using ministry as an opportunity to share how one might be saved. Ministry is not done to make us feel better about ourselves and our church, but to connect people to Jesus. In order to make this connection, we must witness!

<u>Shut-In and Disabled Ministry</u>

- Daily visits to check on
- Make sure medication is taken
- House cleaning
- Run errands

- Meals on wheels
- Helping seniors who are alone with bill paying
- outings
- haircuts and personal hygiene

Construction Ministry

- build ramps for handicapped person at their home
- pick one person per year who needs major house repairs
- Roof repair
- Install a/c window unit or ceiling fans

Collegiate Ministry

- Adopt-a-student
    - call regularly
    - meals at your home
    - respond to requested advice
    - Birthday celebrations
    - Taking them out to eat with your family
- New student welcome – advertised at school and held at church
- Transportation pickup – for church or events in community
- Hold mid-term and finals study hall at the church w/ refreshment
- Provide refreshments, scan-trons (electronic answer sheets) at the school's student center
- Provide a "breakout group" and a contemporary worship service "Friday Night, Saturday Night Live"

Ministry for Jr. Hi and High School

- Auto repairs
- Camshafts for Christ (fellowshipping with students as they learn how to work on cars.
- Kids Hope (adopting a school, connecting Christians with children)

Family Ministries

- Latch-Key (after school care for kids 12 and under who are unsupervised at home until parents get off work
- Mothers' Day Out
- Parent's Night out
- Collection of school supplies
- Support groups (Grief, Divorce and Alcohol (Celebrate Recovery)
- Adoption vs. abortion alternative
- Medical/legal/accounting services
    - – Pregnancy crises
    - – Pre-natal care
    - – Dental clinics
- Life skills classes (applying for jobs, office skills, balancing checkbook
- Young adult cooking class
- Parenting classes
- Abused Spouses support and safe house escapes
- Foster Parents / Adoption

Community Ministries

- Spring Break Backyard Bible Clubs
- On-going backyard Bible clubs (See Children's Traveling Bible Club)

- Community prayer walks
- Thanksgiving feeds
- Children's Traveling Bible Club (puppets, music, Bible stories, lessons and ice cream)
- Fall Festival
- Sports clinics
- Block parties
- Store-front ministries of clothing, food, appliances and furniture
- Bible book studies in home
-

Part 2 – Community Missions

- Fire/police workers relief
- Homeless shelter (providing or working within)
- Job training schools for auto mechanics, childcare and Adult computer literacy
- E.S.L. (English as Second Language)
- Citizenship classes (Isaac Project)
- G.E.D. preparation assistance
- Community health fairs

Special Ministries

- Ministering to individuals and families with A.I.D.s
- Adopt a school to help with the "Christian Club or Bible Club"
- Men's ministry
- Motorcycle ministry
- Help parents with special needs children or gravely ill family members
- Become a hospice volunteer <u>Criminal Justice Ministry</u>

- After-prison, half-way house ministry
  - Housing
  - Education (Christian and public – GED)
  - Befriend an x-offender, mentor him or her in Christ
- Offender Family Ministries
  - Christmas
  - Birthdays of children and spouses

Community Calendar Events

- Local Festivals
- Independence Day festivals
- New Year's events
- Christmas Eve Services (caroling and etc.)
- National Day of Prayer
- Palm Sunday
- Easter Sunday
- Halloween (October 31st)
- Super Bowl parties

Community disaster relief

- THINK OF A NEED and SUPPLY the resource
- Meet with county office of emergency management to discover their needs and how you might assist them
- Consult with Red Cross
- Offer the church as a center for food distribution, disaster relief assessment, or labor forces to help the community with storm or disaster recovery
- Set up short-term housing (Gym or fellowship)

- Arrange donations for food service
- Arrange for volunteers work round-the-clock in the center you have provided
- Arrange transportation (buses to take people to the FEMA or other sites
- Arrange for physicians and counselors to treat those in need
- Absolutely provide a worship and prayer time.
- Provide communications center (email and phone only)
- Provide monitors for local weather

For fire, wind and flood total losses (work with Fire Dept. and other organizations to inform you of the needs

- Have referring agency give the family a voucher
- Contact those that have had the loss and have them come with their voucher and pick out items to meet their needs.
- Open donations for clothing, beds and linens
- Open donations for refrigerators, washers/dryers, tableware and some small items (can openers, microwaves, toasters)

Emergency Room Survival Kits

Have you ever been to an emergency room? Within the four walls are three different types of people: the health care providers, those suffering and the family members waiting for news about their loved ones.

The third group, those waiting, do so minute by minutes, hour by hour sometimes for many hours. Many times, people go to an emergency room go at a moment's notice because of an injury or heart attack. They haven't made plans to go and many times leave for the emergency room without water, snacks or activities to keep restless children pacified.

Our church developed "Emergency Room Survival Kits" to minister to this forgotten need. Our people would go and hand out these kits to people surviving the wait. Here were our approaches:

- Walk up to a person or family and identify ourselves, "Hi, I am Bill. We wanted to come by give you this bag to help you wait out the time until you are able to leave. We want you to know that Jesus loves you, He know where you are and what you're going through.

- We would ask them if they'd like to talk about why they were waiting in the E.R. This wasn't for information, exactly, but more to get them sharing and trying to help them reduce their stress and worry. We found that people were more than ready to share their story.

- Emergency Rooms are not the best place to do evangelism. We would always include a track with our church's name and phone number.

- We would pray for the families or individuals we encountered with a warm comforting hand.

Item we included in the Emergency Room Survival Kits.

Adults

- Snack crackers
- bottled water
- wet wipes
- Kleenex
- paper
- pen
- bite-size candy

Children

- goldfish or animal crackers
- box of apple juice
- bite-size candy (soft only)
- wet wipe
- Kleenex
- paper
- crayons

APPENDIX II

Simple way to plan for ministries outside the four walls of your church.

Here is a simple planning sheet that I have found useful. Much like any other work there will always be things left undone until the last minute or accidentally forgotten. I have used this form for years to help me keep on track. You are welcome to use it too.

Ask yourselves the following questions and begin to complete the Ministry Action Plan (M.A.P.)

Ministry Action Plan

Date:

Purpose:

Personnel Needed

Materials or activities Suggested

Financial Needs and publicity

Space and Time Needs

Helpful Resources to Use

Bible study like any endeavor is as good as your resources. Whether your are a new believer or a more mature follower of Christ, studying the Word of God is essential to your spiritual growth and well-being. Here are some suggestions:

<u>Bible</u>

Pick a reputable translation that you can understand. Understanding God's Word is key to grasping the truths of God. While others around you have their favorite version, some people have chosen a version from traditions. The best translations are the King James Version KJV), the New American Standard (NASB), the New King James Version (NKJV) and the English Standard Version (ESV)

<u>Bible Dictionary</u>

Revell Bible Dictionary is a good, detailed and descriptive with pictures to help you understand and Scripture references.

<u>Commentaries</u>

Sometimes a really good commentary is a great tool to have. Some are highly technical and others are good, but lack a lot of details.

I suggest going to a Christian book store and looking through the commentaries to find one that fits your budget but gives you the details you desire.

Faithlife provides great computer based software, called Logos. There are several packages to meet your needs. They have many different commentaries and they interact with word processors.

www.ingramcontent.com/pod-product-compliance
Lightning Source LLC
LaVergne TN
LVHW051115080426
835510LV00018B/2060